STREAM

and

LIGHT

ALSO BY J. R. NAKKEN:

THREE-POINT SHOT
(FOR YOUNG ADULTS)

STREAM and LIGHT

A Woman's Journey

J. R. Nakken

IMAGO PRESS
TUCSON ARIZONA

Published in the United States of America by:

Imago Press
3710 East Edison
Tucson AZ 85716
www.imagobooks.com

The author and publisher wish to acknowledge publications where portions of this book have appeared previously. The listing may be found on page 219.

Library of Congress Cataloging-in-Publication Data

Nakken, J. R.
  Stream and light : a woman's journey / J.R. Nakken.
    p. cm.
  ISBN-13: 978-0-9799341-6-2 (pbk. : alk. paper)
  ISBN-10: 0-9799341-6-8 (pbk. : alk. paper)
  1. Nakken, J. R. 2. Nakken, J. R.—Childhood and youth. 3. Women—United States—Biography. 4. Recovering alcoholics—United States—Biography. 5. Osceola (S.D.)—Biography. 6. Washington (State)—Biography. I. Title.
  CT275.N2655A3 2008
  973.91092--dc22
  [B]
                2008026088

Author Photograph by Diane Janes
Illustrations © Janet Myer
Book Design by Leila Joiner
Cover Photographs:
      old page of paper © Agnieszka Steinhagen/Fotolia.com
      moissons © Jean-Jacques Cordier/Fotolia.com

ISBN 978-0-9799341-6-2
ISBN 0-9799341-6-8

Printed in the United States of America on Acid-Free Paper

For all the women who have graced my life,
from Big Marge to Little Dorothy,
and especially for Dorcas Leigh.

ACKNOWLEDGMENTS

Special thanks to Richard Loller and the Preservation Foundation for encouragement in the early years of the millennium. I owe an extreme debt of gratitude to Leila Joiner, editor par excellence, for creating a book out of this pile of true stories, and to my Dale, for love, support, and takeout dinners.

J. R. Nakken
Tulalip, Washington
June, 2008

CONTENTS

STREAM

and

LIGHT

FIRST TIME

THE COOL MORNING UNFOLDS AS SHE PLANNED. NEBRASKA'S Septembers are hot, and the old lady's vacant garage sits yards west of her cavernous tan house. It is filled now with the lingering warmth of yesterday afternoon. That heat shimmers on the dust motes, dances with them among piles of boxes, tools, and discarded porch furniture. Her new hideout calls.

She never sees the old lady. Her stepfather goes above and pays the money for living in the basement, but she didn't think Mama ever talked to her. Her mother stayed in the dark apartment with Little Sister all the time, because Father took the car to work. Today she hopes those two women do not see or hear her as she circles the block while the school on the hill calls morning classes. Let the bell ring! She won't do the stupid stuff anymore.

The garage's man door isn't locked, but it's on the side closest to the house. She left it cracked a bit when she secreted the treasure yesterday afternoon, and now her five-year-old heart pounds as she scurries across the asphalt drive and around the corner, through that door. Whew! A sneeze threatens at the dust she raises while removing a piece of carpet that covers the magic chaise.

Future stashes will include Lucky Strikes, Erskine Caldwell, and Four Roses. Today, only *A Tale of Sandy* awaits her. A green apple, a piece of limp cheese, and two of Sister's animal crackers are wrapped in wax paper next to the book. The tiny notebook from Hansen's Grocery waits, a yellow Ticonderoga pencil stub poked through the silver spirals at its top. She stretches, careful of the splintering wicker, and begins to read about Sandy's adventures.

It keeps her mind off school, reading does. But when she stops to list a word she doesn't know—*littered, harnessed, greedy*—or to nibble a bit, the mad rises up and tastes ugly in the top of her throat. In this new town with its red brick prison, they make her sit on the baby side of a partition, while the reading and arithmetic are all on the other side. When the mad turns purple in front of her eyes, she blinks and swallows and reads some more. It calms her; it is a good story, and she plans a trip to the Carnegie Library on Saturday to look up the words. She can't ask Mama; her mother gets real nervous about reading.

The noon bell rings. Mama will expect her home in ten minutes. She rubs her eyes beneath the patched, silver-rimmed spectacles and tucks the notebook in the pocket of her jumper. *A Tale of Sandy* and the chaise are covered again, casually, with the dusty carpet. The young reader congratulates herself as she places her trash in an oily-smelling barrel just inside the door. She is going to ditch school every morning, and thus will never have to color balloons in the dumb kindergarten, ever again.

OSCEOLA

The author says:

We all have childhood comfort spots—places we return to in our daydreams of less complicated days. I have a Nebraska pear tree and an untamed corner of the Hotel Del Coronado's grounds—disparate sanctums that dissipated many a subsequent adult terror.And Osceola. I have Osceola.

It is said you can't go home; that it's best to keep the childhood memory sacrosanct. I write this story of Osceola, of the ambience of its general store, its icehouse, and The Grandpa, to hold out hope to you. Perhaps we can return, if only we're willing to do it often enough.

FATHER WESSMAN'S SHINY GREEN FORD TURNED SOUTH AND slowed. "This is it, Mildred," he said to Mama. "Across from the school." I swiveled my almost-four-year-old head, taking in the sturdy white schoolhouse on my right hand and the small house opposite. He drove into its driveway.

Little Sister snuggled on her half of the scratchy back seat and sucked a couple of times on the thumb in her mouth. I was wide awake and confused. We were going to see The Grandpa-Grandma, and this wasn't where they lived.

"Aren't we going to the farm, Mama? Where the sheep buck beat me up?" I fingered the bumps on my upper lip where the year-old scar was white. It was lumpy inside my mouth, too, and I sometimes thought I could taste the copper penny flavor of blood, but I could no longer remember how bad it once hurt.

Mama was mean today. I didn't think she liked the hot, July drive from Madison. We lived there, upstairs over a noisy place where she worked at night, and our house was hot, too. Little Sister and I had a small bed in a big closet, and we'd lived there since Father Wessman and Mama came to the sheep buck farm and took us away with them, after winter was over.

"They live here now," she told me and pointed up the road. I expanded my gaze in that direction to include a cluster of four or five houses and a brick building with a Nesbitt's Orange Pop sign. Next to that was a gas station, its red flying horse sign unmoving in the heated South Dakota air. "This is their house, and that's Grandpa's store. He's the postmaster here, too."

Mama scrambled out of the car when Grandma came through the screen door to stand on the cement front steps. "You stay with Nancy until she wakes up," she told me.

I got on my knees and looked through the rear window at the schoolhouse. It sat on the opposite corner in the middle of a gravel parking lot, and there wasn't a tree or a flower to be seen. There were two white outhouses in the rear and a merry-go-round in front. I poked Little Sister until she opened her eyes. "There's a merry-go-round across the street," I announced, but just then Grandma came to Little Sister's door and scooped her up.

"Grandma's got cookies," she told us, and then noticed my glasses.

I hated them. They were round and silver and the right one was patched. The whole outside half was covered to make that lazy eye exercise by having to look toward my nose if it wanted to see anything. I didn't mind so much what the glasses looked like, but they bent easily, and Father Wessman had already warned me of the licking I'd get if I broke them. They cost a lot of money.

"Gonna fix that eye, are we?" Grandma crossed her two pointy fingers at me. She did that a lot when we stayed on the sheep buck farm, too, and in this summer of 1940 I didn't know why. I kind of liked it, because it seemed to be special, for me. "That's good. Come on in the house, now."

We walked on the lumpy grass beneath the only tree in the yard, a fat cottonwood. Big, white-painted stones surrounded its scabrous white trunk, and dirt inside the stone circle was nearly invisible beneath the moss roses of every imaginable color that twined there. Their spiky vines seemed to shrink from the searing white rocks, trying to stay cool. Mama loved moss roses and had a little pot of them in our back kitchen window. I guessed I loved them, too.

Still carrying Nancy, Grandma eased the screen door open with her hip. Her black hair was in one braid, wrapped around the back of her head, and her wraparound apron had flour streaks on the sides. She had deep, black eyes that looked right through a little kid. I didn't think she liked me much.

In the house, I looked around for Grandpa. He liked me a lot. "He's down at the store, Judy," Mama answered my searching eyes. "He'll be home for supper."

Father Wessman decided that he and his two girls would go down to see the store and walk home with The Grandpa. Off we went on the path that wound into and then up the borrow pit beside the road. About half a city block it was to the heart of Osceola and Hansen's Grocery.

Osceola, South Dakota was on the prairie, only three generations removed from the virgin, six-foot sod encountered by its first Scandinavian settlers. Dry land farming was the only industry in the countryside, backbreaking work that yielded meager 20-bushel wheat and 40-bushel corn in the rare years that drought or baseball-sized hail didn't erase the year's income. Its eight or nine houses and thirty residents were in Kingsbury County, just this side of the Beadle County line. About a dozen miles east, Laura Ingalls Wilder's little house on the prairie is still celebrated. Twenty-two miles west was Huron, a big city of nine or ten thousand and home to the South Dakota State Fair. Seven miles south, down the steep-sided County Line Road, sprawled Iroquois, a hamlet of three hundred, whose homes were in both counties. A Medal of Honor winner would be born on a farm near there in ten years or so. And in between, in exact mile squares divided by narrow roads of dirt and gravel, was the farmland. Each section had its cluster of red outbuildings and a white house.

Osceola had once been prosperous. The deep, rubble-strewn hole on the right side of the street beside Hansen's store had been a Guarantee State Bank before the recently officially ended Great Depression. Behind Hansen's Grocery stood a large, gray building—gray boards, not gray paint—that was twice as tall on the right side as on the left. Steps and a high porch invited entrance on the tall side, with a regular door down at the other end. This old Opera House, where I was to spend many solitary hours, was abandoned now except for the lower end, in use as the community ice-house. Grain elevators, their metal roofs flashing in the fierce sunshine, loomed a block past the store on the other side of the Great Northern railroad tracks and across from the long, red train depot.

I didn't know any of this yet, in the summer of 1940. I just raised more dust scurrying ahead of my stepfather and Little Sister, anxious to see The Grandpa. When I reached Hansen's Grocery, I hooked my arm around the yellow lantern pole at the corner of the raised cement front porch and swung around it self-consciously, because a kid and his mother were sitting there in the bouncy tin chairs, sharing a pop. I always felt funny around other kids. I finally got my nerve up and burst past them, through the screen door and into the store.

It smelled so good, of cheese and apples and that red, floor-sweeping sawdust stuff. Cigarette smoke and pipe tobacco and a faint odor like the dairy room at the sheep buck farm also filled the air. Glass and silver kerosene lamps hung from the rafters, and a huge pot-bellied stove dominated the middle of the square room. Too big to take down for the summer, I figured. A few dark spots on the wide, oiled floorboards surrounding the stove attested to an occasional hot coal spill. In the winter to come, I would blunder against the red-hot iron and be left with a long, arrowhead-shaped scar on my left forearm, still visible sixty years later. But I would never have changed a thing, if it meant not being in the store with The Grandpa. I loved Hansen's Grocery at first sight and smell.

He was behind the left-hand counter, counting out change to a farmer in a straw hat, and his eyes lit up when he saw me. "Judy, Judy! You've come to stay with Grandpa!" He began to brag to the customer about his oldest granddaughter, "smart as a whip," while I basked in his presence and wondered if it was true. Did I get to stay?

Hans Peter Hansen was a formidable man, big and wide, a gruff son of taciturn Danish immigrants. Born in a sod house there in Kingsbury County in 1883, he was schooled the same way all strapping sons of farmers were: they went to the one-room country schools when they were not needed in the fields of wheat and corn, oats and barley. Usually, they "graduated" eighth grade, and some ventured to Iroquois or De Smet to high school, their spotty attendance forgiven as part of life on the harsh prairie. Grandpa married Zilpha Matheny and raised four daughters on a succession of leased farms in the years from 1905 until he became a storekeeper. My mama was his next-to-youngest girl, the only one who didn't live on a farm within three or four miles of her parents.

I looked the store over good while Grandpa finished with his customer. Straight in front of me was a glass case with long tubes of cold meats, big oblongs of orange cheese, and lots of brown and white eggs. Shelves stocked with canned goods and bread lined the walls behind. In the right-hand corner was the post office, a cubicle of its own whose upper front was made completely of rows of little brass, numbered boxes surrounding a brass grill and counter. Behind the meat and cheese counter was a closed door, and that's all I could see of the room. I read the numbers on the mailboxes, one through sixty, as Grandpa walked the man to the front door and his waiting family. Mama had asked me where I learned to read numbers and little words. I didn't know; one day I just knew how to do it.

Father Wessman and Little Sister were in the store now, and Grandpa and Father shook each other's hand and talked loud to one another. Grandpa gave me a bottle of Nesbitt's Orange to share with Nancy, and said I could look at the back of the store but not to touch a thing. I left her on the counter with the pop to go stand in the door of the post office and marvel. I could see a shiny counter inside under the brass grill, and a small, open wooden box behind each of the numbered doors. Some of the boxes had letters and papers in them. Up against the side wall was a huge, roll-top desk that I could fit under easily, I thought, if I wanted to hide. A long, walk-in safe sat at the far end, its thick, iron door standing open to reveal more pigeonholes and little cubicles. In the spring I was going to experience the mail order chicks that sat in that post office until the farm wives came to town to collect them: stacks of flat, heavy cardboard boxes with round holes in the sides, alive with downy yellow and the endless peeping of baby birds. I would lie beside them, filling my fingertips with their softness, and coo back at them for hours at a time.

I opened the closed door behind the meat counter. This was where the dairy odor came from. Silver cream cans and big egg crates lined the cool walls, and there was a long counter with test tubes, shiny equipment, and piped-in water from the good artesian well out back. Here, Grandpa would teach me about centrifugal force, as the tubes filled with cream rotated in the testing equipment. The price of cream depended upon the butterfat content, he would tell me; when the tubes were through whirling, the notches on the side told him what that content was. Every day, the dairy truck came from Huron to pick up the eggs and cream that Grandpa had brokered for the farmers, and then he paid them. Sometimes, he gave them money, but usually he asked if he could "put it on the bill." The bills were fold-over books of tickets beside the Copenhagen rack at the main counter—one for each family that traded at Hansen's Grocery.

Outside the cream room's slab door stood the outhouse, a discreet distance behind the well. Across a former alleyway was the old Opera House. The weeds were already brown and high against the gray of the icehouse, but across the side street I could see green trees surrounding a huge, unpainted house. Its garden was ablaze with midsummer flowers, the clumps separated by iron tools that were antique even then: a dozen boot scrapers shaped like different animals, a harness maker's bench, and huge, cast-iron pots for catching rainwater from South Dakota's sudden, violent rainstorms.

Ed Currier was an ancient man, and the inside of his home was to prove a boon to my early education. His collection of Native American artifacts, picked up right there on the Osceola prairie, was unparalleled by most of today's small museums. Hundreds of arrowheads were mounted on felt boards in his living quarters, some smaller than a dime, and ax heads with rope-worn grooves made a pile by the wood stove. He wove stories around the willow backboard and the birch travois that stood against his parlor wall.

Ed cherished his trees and his garden. The only trees in this part of the country were the occasional cottonwood, its stubborn seed probably dropped by a bird, or rows of planted windbreaks whose owners had to be willing to lavish time and water on them. Ed spent all his outside time with buckets of water, but always had time for a glass of lemonade with a polite child.

The Ford and my family were gone when I arose from the floor bed Grandma made me that first night. She hugged and kissed me and gave me a cookie for breakfast and talked about my birthday next week, July 23. I stayed in the house with her that day, but every other day I went to Hansen's Grocery with The Grandpa.

It was a nice house. The main part was two rooms, open to one another with colonnades between to separate the parlor from the kitchen. A kerosene lamp hung above the round oak table in the kitchen, and clear glass lamps stood on the table and beside Grandpa's chair in the living room. Grandma heated the curling iron for my long curls by poking it down in the lamp chimney. The kitchen boasted a huge, oak icebox. Grandma was always willing to stab a sliver of ice from the block that lay in the lower compartment, her green-handled ice pick flashing as she chipped something cool for me to suck. Yesterday, she had bragged to Mama about her shiny, bottled-gas stove. "The wood stove's in the basement and never coming back up here," she vowed.

The pantry floor lifted up and became the entrance to the basement! It was about 4 x 8 and hooked to the side to reveal steep stairs and a musty odor. A large, brick cistern for catching rainwater dominated the basement room. A pump at the square kitchen sink in front of the back yard window brought cistern water upstairs for boiling and bathing, but not for drinking. Grandpa brought jugs of water from the store for that. Two bedrooms completed the solid, square house that would not have electricity until 1946 or an indoor bathroom until 1950, long after Grandma's untimely death. Even without a bathroom, I loved it.

I counted the days until the weekly grocery shipment arrived on the Galloping Goose. The Goose, a train with a big, leaping goat on its engine, came through Osceola every day, although it didn't always stop. Some days, the depot agent put the mailbag on a tall contraption beside the station, and some other contraption on the train would reach out and—whoosh!—grab the bag. When the section crews worked on the tracks, Grandpa would take me with him to eat supper in their dining car. The dishes were thick, like restaurant plates, but not ugly, and there was as much food as my aunts prepared for the threshing crews.

I tended the store while Grandpa wheeled the big handcart down to the depot's long wooden platform and loaded our order. Bananas came in baby-coffin-sized, blackened wooden boxes whose lids had to be prized off. The stalks were as tall as I was. In the summer we always had to keep a couple of fragile cardboard boxes of candy bars in the ice-cooled meat counter, and Grandpa always slipped me one, like it was a secret he was stealing from himself. I dusted with the feather duster before I put new cans away.

The Grandpa was proud of two things. He didn't have to weigh anything, and his blood was black. "Half a pound," he would announce. "Watch this." His big knife would slice the cheese or bologna in one whack, and, when he placed it with the waxed paper into the silver-scoop scales, it was never a quarter of an ounce off. I learned how to write the abbreviations in the books that summer when I was four— bol, chs, cndy—and could wait on customers who put their purchases on the bill. Grandpa would list the prices later. He bragged on me to everyone who came in. "My four-year-old clerk will help you," he'd say with a grin. "She's a real smart one."

On the rare occasion that he skinned a knuckle or cut himself, The Grandpa displayed the seepage to anyone who would look. His blood really was so dark as to appear black, and flowed ever so slowly from a cut or scrape. It was, of course, harbinger of the arteriosclerosis that was to end his life.

The summer passed. I got a book and a green dress for my fourth birthday. Grandma made a cake, and Grandpa froze a big tub of ice cream. All three aunts and uncles and my two boy cousins, Gale and Gene, came. We played on the merry-go-round across the street, and I threw up from too many root beer floats. Cousin Gale talked about coming to town to school pretty soon. He was going to be in the fourth grade. Gene was only three, but about as big as me.

Sure enough, after the Labor Day celebration, the kids came to school across the street. Grandma said I couldn't go over, so I stood in the borrow pit and peeked at them when they played outside. The schoolteacher had a black Model A, and she stayed in the school building all week, driving back to Huron on Friday after school. The cottonwood leaves were floating in the air when I first ran away to school.

I waited until after the bell rang and crept quietly up the inside steps. On the right side was the classroom, where all twelve children got to read and write and stuff. Alongside the classroom was a long, narrow cloakroom. I was hiding at the end of the jackets, listening to the reading and counting, when Grandma came to get me. She and the teacher laughed

and patted me, and said I had to go home. But I went back to the cloakroom whenever I could escape Grandma's baleful eye. Mrs. Long soon began to look for me in the mornings, and would lead me to the front door of the school, pat my fanny and send me home.

She came to supper once. Grandma had pheasant in gravy (we ate it year 'round, as the fields were always in motion with their ring-necked beauty; when it was not hunting season, we called it stubble duck) and an apple pie. I read and wrote numbers for Mrs. Long, and she went home across the street when Grandpa began to listen to "The Lone Ranger."

It was frosty the next time I hid in the cloakroom; there were more coats and sweaters to hide in, but she found me, anyway. She was not mean, but today Mrs. Long stood in the doorway of the narrow aperture in her stocky black dress, her hand held out. I was scared at this departure from our morning routine.

"Come on, Judy. I have a desk for you." She escorted me into the classroom where sat a dozen other children from six to fourteen, and my first grade education began. I learned of Washington and Lincoln and Old Ironsides and Rosa Bon-heur, and to sing songs like *My Country 'Tis of Thee, Solomon Levi* and *Beautiful Dreamer*. Bigger words came easy with tutelage, and I read everything I could get my hands on. Mrs. Long let me take books across the street, but Grandma made a rule about no reading at meals and none after dark. The kerosene light was just not good for my eyes, she explained.

I missed being at the store with The Grandpa, of course, but I ran down there nearly every afternoon. One day, he had a secret box from the Galloping Goose shipment. I teased him all the way home to supper about what was in the box.

He assembled it at the kitchen table after we ate. It was a Coleman lantern! When its two, flimsy wicks were combusted, it seemed to turn the nighttime kitchen into day. "Now you can read after supper if you want to," he told me. He didn't hug a lot, but The Grandpa really loved me.

I had investigated the old Opera House that first summer. There was a high peg on the icehouse door, but two kids could get it open if they wanted to, and sometimes, when it was real hot, we went in just to lie on the cold, damp straw that insulated the slabs of ice. The upper door wasn't locked. Inside was a giant black piano on a broken-down stage, and remnants of wooden chairs that hooked together. I sat alone at that old grand piano many, many hours, coaxing an occasional sound from the dilapidated keys and pretending I made music. My mama played the piano.

There was a blizzard before Christmas, and no one got to town for three days except Santa Claus. I put all the little candles in their shiny tin holders and clipped them carefully on the Christmas tree branches, but Grandma wouldn't let us light them. She was too afraid of starting a fire. Then it was midwinter, time to fill the empty icehouse. All the farmers came on Saturday to Lake Osceola, built during the depression by the WPA to give employment to the jobless. They drove teams of big horses, not long retired to their pastures by International and John Deere tractors. The teams loved having something to do. Aunt Loie's Doc and Don pranced and kicked up like colts as they pulled a stone boat. All the town men went out to the lake, too, for it took a lot of cross-cut sawing and ice-tonging to load the 2 x 4 blocks onto the flat-runnered, wooden stone boats, and more manpower to drive the teams back to town and unload the ice. Everyone who used it in the summer months worked to gather the several tons of ice. As load after load of ice blocks were removed, I worried that there would be no lake left to swim in when next summer came!

The women had their work on ice harvest day, also. The sloping gravel from the bathhouse to the water always had a couple or three cars with women and children bringing hot coffee and sandwiches, and sometimes cocoa for us kids. It was like a big party, but even at four and a half I knew how important it was. The ice had to last us all the next summer. When that next summer came, I had a different feeling for the icehouse. It wasn't a playhouse. It was too special, and I didn't sneak in there anymore.

They came to the Labor Day picnic in the round, green '39 Ford, not so shiny as it had been, and took me away from Osceola. Mama hugged me a lot and called me her big girl. Nancy squeezed under my arm and sat close to me every chance she got. I told them Grandpa really needed me in the store and cried all the way to North Bend, Nebraska when they wouldn't listen.

In North Bend we lived in a dark basement, and I was enrolled in kindergarten as the school laws prescribed, having just had my fifth birthday. Right there in that baby-stuff kindergarten, I became the discipline problem I would not outgrow until I was forty years old.

Morse Bluff, Nebraska and Watertown, South Dakota schools followed, for World War II was roaring and Father Wessman had steady work. When Grandma died, we went to Auntie Ev's farmhouse at Christmastime, where everyone was crying, and Grandpa didn't want to talk to me. After we went back home, I tried to run away to Osceola. Father, in the green Ford, caught me on a country road and said I was going in the wrong direction.

I don't know what circumstances sent us all to Osceola again in 1945. We lived in the little square house with Grandpa for most of two years. It was crowded, for we now had Baby Keeto, but I was overjoyed. Father dug a well and wired the house and the store and the auntie's farms for Delco Plant electricity, for no one knew when the Rural Electrification Agency's utility poles were going to get this far out. Now we had a refrigerator and ice cream at Hansen's Grocery! Mrs. Long still taught in one room of the schoolhouse and lived in another, and there were Erickson and Odom kids, my age, behind me in school because I had skipped grades in Nebraska. Grandpa ordered books for me, twice a month, from the traveling library. They were mailed all the way from Pierre, the state capitol. I spent a week painstakingly removing all the "ivory" from the Opera House piano and presented it proudly to Mama, only to see it go up in flames when she threw a kitchen match into the pitiful pile of celluloid I deposited in the back yard. Kenny Erickson quit me for a little, blonde first-grader who kissed better than I did, and Father Wessman got his final job in Iroquois. We moved for the last time, as a family, in a maroon '38 Chevy. The green Ford had given up its ghost.

I went back to Osceola in 1975, and the sight broke my heart. The town was virtually abandoned. The train tracks were overgrown, and the depot was rusty with disuse. Hansen's Grocery had been renovated into a garage with a corrugated metal overhead door before it burnt out; now, only scattered bricks remained. Rural electrification finally happened in

1948, so the icehouse was gone. The weeds grew tall where Ed Currier's home and gardens had been, and Mrs. Long's schoolhouse was a pile of rubble. In the countryside, all the aunties' farm buildings were disintegrating. Mennonites from the colony near Iroquois were diligently coaxing bountiful crops from lands my uncles had "soil banked," but their mode of communal living brooked no use for the buildings. I looked at row after row of hames and harness in the top of Uncle Gib's tall red barn and remembered the horse-powered threshing machines and magnificent meals I'd had there during harvest. I took a stone or a brick from everywhere I had loved, and was sorry I returned.

Thus it was tarnished, my childhood happy place, in the middle years of my memory. Grandpa had married again and died Out West in the mid-sixties, and I had no reason to think I would ever return. But Y2K fever infected Iroquois High School alumni, and they had an impressive all-class reunion in July, 2000. Nancy and I attended from the Pacific Northwest.

"You live in Osceola, don't you?" my cousin, Gene, asked the waitress in the neat little roadside café on Highway 14. "Where 'bouts?"

She giggled, notwithstanding her plain clothes, and replied, "One place north of the dirt house!"

Gene explained that one of the Mennonite settlers now living there had built a house, and then covered it with earth for ecological purposes. One house north, he went on, was our grandfather's old home.

It was twenty-five years since my last, unhappy visit, and I turned off the County Line Road with a pounding heart. I saw trees and gardens, a church and a school, and my eyes were misting even before we made the last corner and saw

The Grandpa's solid white house. The cottonwood was now a giant, still ringed with stones, and a hill of dirt with windows did, indeed, loom just beyond it. Mrs. Ada Odom still lived across the back field, about to celebrate her ninetieth birthday, and there was an addition to the field.

The Great Northern Depot, strangely shrunken, but repainted in red splendor with its square, black-lettered OSCEOLA screaming at the countryside, sat in front of Odom's compound. "They were going to tear it down," the spry old gal told us, "and my Gil, God rest his soul, couldn't stand it. He put it up on skids and hauled it down here. And here it will stay."

And here they will stay, my final memories of Osceola. Children play, Monday washes hang on summer clotheslines, and the Great Northern depot sits in a trackless field forever. The spirit of home is undaunted, sure to be revived in each generation or two. Sometimes, perfect times, you really can return.

IVORY SWAN

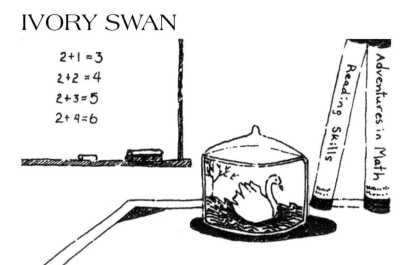

$2 + 1 = 3$
$2 + 2 = 4$
$2 + 3 = 5$
$2 + 4 = 6$

THE HOMEMADE PRESENT FOR MISS RACZEK WAS LIGHTWEIGHT, wrapped in crisp tissue paper Mama ironed between tea towels this morning. I scuffed my overshoes slowly up the hill and examined each Nebraska snow bank I passed. I could bury it and just not take a gift. But if Mama found out, she'd tell Father! I shuddered with more than December cold.

I put a hex on the package, stared at it with my half-patched right eye, hoping to turn it into candy or hankies. My grandma, who died last year up in South Dakota, believed that walleyed girls were witches. I think my mama believes it, too. She watches me when she thinks I'm not looking. But I was now at the yawning maw of the brick, two-story school, and I could still hear the old glassine powder box, noisy under the tissue paper. So what good was it being an ugly little seven-year-old witch if I couldn't turn this into something else?

I was committed when I reached the door to the room where first, second, and third grades met. Miss Raczek stood there, receiving hankies or proud, rare fruit and candies from other children. Shortages were the rule in this second full year of the war against old Hitler and Mussolini. Most fruits and all candy were noticeably absent from the grocer's shelves.

She smiled big at me. She always did, because I knew she felt sorry for me. Her freckled arm reached for my package, and I had to let her have it. I thrust it at her and scurried to my seat with the third graders, who chattered to one another in Czech as I arrived.

They weren't bigger than me, the third graders. I was big for my age, as well as smart. We'd only been in Morse Bluff since August, but I understood a lot of their Bohemian words already. *Eyes. Great Big Head.* I was the only real American kid in the whole school until a few weeks ago, and they shunned me. I didn't care.

Mama and Miss Raczek said I was going in the next room to the fourth grade after Christmas vacation. Some of those sixth graders in that room were as big as Miss Raczek, and I had just moved up to the third grade at Halloween. I wanted to go, though. In the next room, they had maps that pulled down and a full set of purple encyclopedias angled into a bookcase. And they could check out fat books from the library in the high school upstairs if they wanted to, but I didn't think they wanted to very often.

Miss Raczek called for order in her vibrant voice, her square face plain and sweet. She was never mean to any kid, yet they all obeyed her. As I looked at her I thought of my beautiful mama with faint freckles under her face makeup and brown ones on her arms. When Miss Raczek was a mother, her kids would think she was the most beautiful person in the world, because that's the way it was with children and their mothers. Jessie Ann's mother was plain ugly, like Dogpatch. It was hard for me to believe Jessie Ann's eyes saw her as pretty as my mama was, but I knew it was so. I couldn't wait to get my own kids and be beautiful.

"Come to order now!" Miss Raczek waved her hands in the general direction of all those not seated. "I know you want me to open these gifts, and I will do so if you will take out yesterday's reading material and review it." She started to open flat boxes of store-bought handkerchiefs and thicker ones of candy.

The room began to assume the odor of oranges and chocolate and resounded with the lifting and closing of desks, the rustling of pages. As she read each card or note, my teacher wrote a line on her tablet. Probably to call the mothers, I figured, and thank them. What on earth could she say to my mother? *Thank you for the cheap soap?*

Oh, no! She was taking the tissue paper off my present, reading the burnt-edged paper note attached.

Wade Bell was not studying. He was making comments to everyone around him. He was eight and in the second grade, littler than me and always dirty. I avoided him in the cloakroom because his short black hair stank, and I was afraid it would rub off if he touched me. I already knew he had my name in the drawing and agonized over what gift I might get from him. All the Christmas presents were piled under the big tree in the auditorium. They'd be passed out after the program tonight.

I went to Wade's house when they first moved here. My mama sent me with a plate of cookies. His dad did War Work with my father, and they rode together to save coupons. The Bell's house was smelly, too full of dogs and little kids and his mother in her underwear. They gobbled up the cookies, kids and dogs alike, and didn't even offer me one. I told Mama I didn't want to go back, and she said it was okay. Wade was the other American kid in school.

His beady black eyes were dancing as he pointed and whispered. "Looky. Somebody half burned up their card! Looky!" One grubby hand indicated Miss Raczek's desk. She was reading inside the folded paper my mother had toasted brown in the oven and singed around the edges with matches.

"Silence, class, silence! Or we will do our arithmetic instead of opening gifts." The room hushed. Of course, it would be just when she removed that old, cheap powder box from the used tissue paper. They all saw it. I scrunched down and made myself invisible.

The dome was punched inward on one side, probably from my thrust at the classroom door. Miss Raczek touched gently at one side and then the other of the cavity, trying to make it pop out. The crackling thundered in the room of forty eyes, forty ears.

When her poking didn't work, she sat it in front of her and lifted the see-through cover straight up, careful not to disturb the homemade water in the box. She stroked the inside of the lid gently and replaced it. It was now smooth and clear and you could see the scene from all sides. Miss Raczek twirled the box slowly and looked faraway, like Mama sometimes did when she rubbed powder on the baby.

The water was made from cotton balls soaked in bluing, then dried and pulled about. It raged wildly on the surface of the powder box pond, trying to flood out, trying to upset the soap that sat in its middle and the three little weeds glued to one side of the dome. Half a seven-cent bar of Ivory soap it was, now a swan with its neck arched and wings furled.

It could have been a pure white kitten, a lion, an owl, or a bear in a whole forest of weeds. All the shelves and most of the bay window seat in our dining room were covered with soap animals exactly the size of a half bar of Ivory. The whole house smelled like soap. If Mama didn't like the finished result, or if they broke a leg or a wing, my baby brother got them in the washtub for his suppertime bath in the warm kitchen. Keeto loved his floating animals.

When I was little I liked to watch her carve the bar with the big and little paring knives, to see the animals appear as the soap chipped away and to help her capture the flakes for washing dishes. The smallest lines and holes were made with the orange sticks she also used to fix her fingernails. But now I wanted to be just a regular kid, whose mom yelled and worked in the garden and hung over the back fence with Mrs. Vopolinsky. I wanted to live in an American town, to not wear glasses, to be like other kids and have a real present for my teacher!

The dreamy look faded from Miss Raczek's face. She took her hand from the box and began to record furiously on the tablet. *She is probably trying to think of something nice to say to my mother; she's so sweet,* I thought. She opened the rest of the hankies and candy, and you could tell which kid's package was being unwrapped by the proud looks. I stayed invisible, turning myself into Tess in the Limberlost. I was reading it at home.

Miss Raczek finished opening the gifts. We did some arithmetic for a while and were then dismissed for vacation at noontime. The whole school would come back at seven that night for the Christmas program and the presents. My mama already said she'd try to come. I was saying *The Night Before Christmas* by heart.

Miss Raczek waved me into the corner by the door as she bid good-bye to the other twenty children. "Thank you, thank you!" She beamed at everyone and adjusted scarves and hats as they left the cloakroom to go into the pale day. Alone with her, I was ashamed. She was going to be nice to me again.

"Judy. Will your mother be at the program tonight?"

"She said she'd try, Miss Raczek." Was I going to get off this easy? No, I wasn't.

"Judy. Please tell your mother that the swan diorama is the most beautiful thing I have ever owned. I'll treasure it always. Please ask her to come tonight, so I can tell her myself." I'd look up diorama when I was alone in the schoolroom; I didn't want her to know I didn't know what the word meant.

She went on lying, going overboard in her praise. She always tried to make me feel good, and I was sick of Miss Raczek. She was still adjusting the scarf around the stiff plaid jacket that matched my snow pants when I escaped out the door.

Tears did not freeze on my cheeks as they did in the storybooks. I wiped them all away before I reached the bottom of the hill. "She said to tell you 'thanks,'" I told Mama when she asked about the swan.

I didn't look for my mother in the audience like little kids do. I knew she wasn't there. She'd made long curls of my hair and let me go without my glasses in my red dress, and said she would try to come. She walked me to the door and waited until other families were walking up the dark hill to the lighted schoolhouse before she let me go out. I said my piece perfectly. Miss Raczek clapped and clapped.

The teachers gave the principal a gift, and he talked for a long time. Finally, he began to pass out the presents stacked under the tree. Kids around me were either ripping into their presents or teasing their folks to let them if their parents insisted that the pretty boxes go home under the tree until Christmas morning. Wade Bell's mother wasn't there, either, and he opened his present. It was a box of at least eight paints with two brushes and a book to paint in.

Almost everyone had their present, and people were making noise with their chairs. I squirmed on my wooden seat. A couple of big boys were snapping gift scarves at each other, and then there were two kids who did not have a gift and only one package left under the tree. I knew the truth before the little man with the thick glasses called Jerry Chalupsky's name. Wade Bell hadn't brought me a present.

The principal waved his hand at his high school assistant, and she went behind the podium and got a red, rattling box. "Judy Roberts," he called.

It was a big-piece puzzle, and on the bottom of the box it said 1-2-3 in black crayon. A picture of the wooden space it had come from flashed in my head. It must still contain boxes marked 4-5-6 and 7-8, in case someone in those rooms didn't get a present. I made a picture in my head of the snow bank where I'd bury the baby puzzle on the walk home. I was drawing a picture in my head of Wade's face pounded to a bloody mess just as Miss Raczek stopped me from slipping out the side exit.

"Judy, please tell your mother again how much…" A long, strange look came into her eyes, and I jerked out of her grasp and ran, fell, and ricocheted into piled snow at the side of the walk. I hated her and all Bohemians and Americans and my mother. I brushed at my clothes and did not cry.

Thirty-something years later, I picked up a four-pack of Ivory at the grocery for no reason and was deluged with the first tears of my adult life. The soap's odor triggered my childhood heart. I stood in the aisle and wept as I realized what that long-ago teacher's gaze portended. One day, I would recognize the rare talent, the beauty alive in that kitchen-carved swan, and she hoped it would not be too late.

I like to think Miss Raczek and my mother are watching me from somewhere when I buy the occasional bar of this particular soap as I do the shopping for my solitary life. I break it here at the typewriter table, and the chips remain until they are scentless. I lift the half bar often and inhale deep memories of Ivory bears and lions. The scent of one particular swan is sharp in my nostrils. Sometimes, I brush the soap crumbs from the table and float them with occasional tears in the evening's dishwater. When I return to the keyboard, I finish another self-help article about taking a risk, reaching out, examining false truths, learning to communicate. And I hope you hear me.

ALL-AMERICAN BOY

It was after four o'clock in Watertown, a weekday in April, 1945. School kept from nine until four, and all the Johnnies could read. I know what time it was because I was stretched out on my stomach in front of the radio after school, listening to "Jack Armstrong, the All-American Boy."

The radio was Father's prize possession. It sat on the floor at the end of the scratchy sofa, next to his wood and leather platform rocker. I dusted it every Saturday. I knew the grain of the walnut and the smell of the dusty cloth in the center and the intricacies of its name—Motorola—that had to be cleaned with a bobby pin. The square glass on the top with its rounded corners must always be free of fingerprints. I polished it every night when my programs were over, before Father got home.

The scarred, upright piano was Mama's favorite thing. She played it in the morning after Father went off to do his War Work. Her feet danced on the pedals, and she swung on the stool as she played the tunes of the day. "Mister Whatchacallit, Whatcha doin' tonight?" she sang, as she played without music. Mama was happy at the piano.

News flashes interrupted too many of my programs these days. We were whipping Hitler's ass off in France and bombing the hell out of Germany, and the radio guys told us in great detail about every victory. On this April 12th, they interrupted again. I indulged myself in more cuss words, since Father wasn't around. Then the day's bulletin began to seep into my precocious eight-year-old brain.

…at Warm Springs, Georgia, the radio announcer intoned. *He was pronounced dead…President Roosevelt was 63.* My head was spinning. Did presidents die, like grandmas? FDR had been president forever. I ran upstairs.

Our rented, white asbestos-sided house resembled every other prewar house in the Midwest. It sat near the edge of this city of eight thousand, across the street from the hospital where my little sister had not died from a ruptured appendix a few months ago in a day when antibiotics were still a futuristic dream. There was a vacant lot on one side, where neighbor kids played baseball in nice weather, and a mom and pop grocery on the corner, where I could trade two scavenged pop bottles for a nickel ice cream cone.

You entered our house through a small enclosure that protected the front door against the frigid prairie winters: a bare-floored cabin of its own for leaving boots and wet clothes and other items Father didn't want in the house. Its windows didn't open, so it was unbearable in the entry on hundred-degree summer days.

A heavy oak door opened inward onto the dark wood of the hall floor. The parlor was on the left beyond a sliding door. Straight down the narrow hallway was the kitchen. The staircase to the bedrooms ran steeply up along the right-hand wall.

The bathroom at the top of the stairs had once been either a large walk-in linen closet or a very small nursery. I could see my claustrophobic mama standing in front of the mirror with the door open, taking bobby pins from her hair and placing them in the little gold scrolled glass jar that had been my grandma's. I had a shiver of *deja vu* as I stood on the landing with my news.

Last fall, they let the whole school out to go down to the main street. Thomas E. Dewey talked to us from the back of a big farm truck that sported an American flag. Two round rag rugs overlapped on the floorboards; some folding chairs sat up front, and some leaned in corners at the back of the flatbed.

Didn't our teacher say he was the new president? I didn't really hear his words, just watched the people on the truck and clapped when they did. I liked the way Mr. Dewey sat on the end of the truck and swung his legs over, just like a real person.

I ran all the way home and raced up the stairs. "Mama, Mama!" I called, breathless with excitement. "Mama, I saw President Dewey just now!"

Her beautiful face became witchlike in an instant, and she struck before I could leap away. Smack! The side of my face stung, and my ear rang as I clung to the newel post to keep from tumbling back down the stairs. "Never! Never!" she screeched as she tried to reach me with her striking right hand while holding on to her bobby pin box with the left. "Never! What an ugly little girl thing to say!"

But that was then. Now our president—our real president—was dead. "Mama," I purposely subdued my excitement. "Mama, President Roosevelt just died."

Witchlike, her face, and the smack happened again, without warning. She didn't try to protect her mother's precious glass box as she hit me. This time I did fall, accompanied by her screams of refusal to accept the idea of FDR's death.

"Don't *ever* say that, Judy Roberts!"

I sniveled as I listened to the last of Jack Armstrong and wondered about this other All-American Boy, Roosevelt, who held my mother in thrall. What was it about a man my mother didn't even know, had never set eyes on, that ignited such passion in her usually passive self? I didn't understand, but even in my young misery I admired her loyalty to the man. The feeling served me well in succeeding years when her timid vanity, viewed through my feminist nature, caused me to dislike her intensely. I'd call up the memory of that loyalty as an asset, something to be proud of in my mother, and the teenaged disgust I directed at her would abate for the moment.

The bottom dropped out of my maternal respect bucket the day I discovered that my stepfather was the ardent Democrat. My mother had never registered or cast a vote. I was soon gone from home, and it was a dozen years before I had occasion to speak to her again.

I called her on November 22, 1963, the day they killed my president. JFK, the boy for all America, was chopped down in the prime of his presidency, most of his material promises unfulfilled. My grief was inconsolable. I felt as if America the Beautiful had died, though I, too, had never voted.

PRINCE MONK

THERE WERE THIRTY-NINE TEENAGERS IN THE HIGH SCHOOL upstairs, that autumn of 1947. Seventy-four noisy students received their primary education in four classrooms on the first floor. I was not yet twelve years old and in the 8th grade, with an unbelievable IQ, one lazy eye, and two white cotton brassieres, size 36-D.

Monk, on the other hand, was sixteen and in the 7th grade. His family had moved often during the war years, and the older children were all two or three grades behind. He was a lanky six feet, with short, blond hair, perpetually red-rimmed eyes, and green teeth. A happy soul was Duane-called-Monk—a poor student and a good sport.

Homecoming was a week from Saturday night. On this day, the ritual choosing of King and Queen candidates was happening upstairs in each of the four high school classes. Each of the lower grade rooms would also choose candidates for their Prince and Princess.

We would sell tickets for twelve days, ten cents apiece, three for a quarter. Each classroom would turn in its money a week from Friday, and we would know who the royalty were before we went home from school. All the couples would be honored, and the ticket sales winners crowned the next night. There were no sports at Homecoming, only a program and dance in the gym. The two royal pairs would reign over the evening.

Twelve days was plenty in this South Dakota prairie town of three hundred souls. The Homecoming royalty was never a surprise. Townspeople bought the tickets to support the extra-curricular school equipment the monies purchased, and they always bought them from the high school seniors and for the prince and princess from first and second grades. The pair from the graduating class and the little kids always got the crowns.

Lowell and Doody were our candidates last year. They were a dismal fourth in ticket sales. He was a freshman this year, but Doody was still in our classroom, and she was vocal all week. "Don't nominate me! I won't parade around in my long dress again!"

Our teacher opened Princess nominations first. Clare Sorheim put my name forward. Why? He hated me. He complained that my scores ruined tests graded on the curve. He and Blub Stoneking had hid my crutches the previous winter, and lied about it to everyone but me. His gesture today was so extraordinary it invaded the private world I inhabited most of the time.

Someone seconded Clare's nomination immediately, amid a buzz of quiet chatter and stifled giggles. Our teacher had to insist on one more candidate. When the other girl and I returned to the room, Miss Ramsell was wearing her fake face. "Judy Roberts! You are our Princess candidate. Congratulations!"

It was a conspiracy, of course. The room quickly acclaimed Monk my prince. He was good-natured about it, grinning at the razzing he took from the boys. I retreated into my library book and vowed silently to sell no tickets.

Mama was proud. "I'll make you a sweet little long dress," she said. I was not consoled. I had been bigger than she for a year now, and nothing 'sweet' was ever going to look good on me.

It was dotted Swiss: little white dots on velvety red. There was a high, wide scoop neck outlined with a two-inch ruffle. The ruffle was edged in narrow thread lace. "Plenty of seam under here, honey," my mama said. "To pin your bra straps." A matching ruffle surrounded the floor-length, gathered skirt about halfway between my knees and the floor.

I won the battle of the waistline. She wanted it gathered, full, with a sash of—you guessed it—dotted Swiss edged in white lace. I pleaded for an inset band, like Wonder Woman's belt, and no sash. The waistline just saved my dress from 'sweet.' Barely.

"It's not polite to vote for yourself," I told my stepfather when he asked me why I hadn't hit him up to buy tickets. "Buy some from Keeto. The little kids should win." My little brother was in first grade.

It was a year of upsets, upstairs and down. Wendell and Eleanor, starry-eyed junior class sweethearts, were going to be king and queen. And Miss Ramsell's room sold more tickets than any other, for the first time in recorded history.

If I weren't lucky enough to die before Saturday night, I would reign over Homecoming with my frog prince. My Monk prince. And if I did die, my mama would probably dress my body in dotted Swiss and wheel it on an appliance

dolly to the festivities, she was that proud. She burned up
the telephone wires Friday night, making sure relatives in
neighboring towns came to see me crowned.

It was unbelievable that she could not see the cruel joke
of it. Indeed, she went to her grave telling about how her
Judy was the Homecoming Princess. It was my first lesson
about life and living being all a matter of perception.

I had to be at the gymnasium early, so Father gave me a
ride to save wear and tear on the new dress. Our married but
spinsterish music teacher was responsible for the royal processional, and she put us through our paces in her no-nonsense
manner. "Grace and dignity, people. With…grace…and…
dignity." She soon had us shaped up enough to promenade
in our finery.

Monk looked really nice in gray dress pants, a dark suit
coat, and yellow tie. His eyes were still red-rimmed, but his
gap-toothed grin dazzled. Neither of us seemed to know
left foot from right, and we got the giggles on the first run-
through. Mrs. Schultz censured us sharply, and we were soon
glissading comfortably with the rest of the royalty.

The makeshift room at the left of the stage was for the
girls. It had a full-length mirror at which feminine royalty
could primp. "It's a real pretty dress, Judy," said the queen-
elect as we stood in line to use it. She was gorgeous and kind,
as usual, adding some rosebud lipstick to her already-perfect
mouth and moving away quickly. I stepped up to see if my
inch-wide bra straps showed.

In a slick piece of fiction, this is the moment when
someone who looked like Jane Russell, that year's "Outlaw"
sex symbol, would gaze back from the mirror. But real life
is all about perception, remember, and only fifty-year-old

photographs tell me that story. As the piano processional began, all I saw in the mirror was the reflection of a lumpy girl with six hooks on her white cotton bra and the dumbest, ugliest loser in the world for a prince.

We flowed with grace and dignity, beginning with the tiny, blonde first-grader, and met our consorts at center stage. Each couple stood for applause and moved downstage to walk the aisle and back. When Monk extended his arm for me the way Mrs. Schultz had showed us, laughter and some catcalls erupted amid the applause. He stopped for a split second, stiffened his back and purposefully did the arm thing again. I took it, and we glided through our paces alone to applause. My lightweight dress floated airily down the steps and across the floor.

Back on stage, the master of ceremonies made the pronouncements. Prince and Princess were first. Silver cardboard crowns were placed on my dark head, his fair one. Monk held a silvered, pool-cue scepter, and I got a red wax rose. We stood at the front of the stage with the King and Queen in their golden crowns and held court until the music started. I had already popped out of reality when last year's little princess stretched to put the crown on my head, and only returned from my reverie at the sound of his mother's voice.

Her red-rimmed eyes were so like his, and wet. "You did just perfect, son," she gushed. "Just like I asked you to. You're a fine boy, and you even *look* like a prince!" She wanted to hug and kiss him but didn't; just cried a little more and backed away into the crowd.

I was more at ease with him now that the ordeal was over. Anyway, this charade wasn't his fault. I tried to make conversation. "My mom didn't tell me anything. What did your mother tell you, Monk?"

He stammered and blushed, reverted to mumbling Monk, and then gave me my second lesson on life as a matter of perception. "Well, it doesn't mean anything now, Judy. It's really been okay. You're not so bad, after all. But at first I...well... she told me to treat you like a princess. Even though I knew the whole thing was just a big joke on me."

BEER BUS

The author says:

This true story was a writing exercise: Tell a complete story in twenty-six sentences, with the first letter of each sentence in alphabetical order. Student's names have all been changed, protecting the miscreants and innocents alike.

"A FINE HOWDY-DO," MOANED RAY, IROQUOIS HIGH SCHOOL's janitor/bus driver, to Coach and Miss Ramsell. Boys and girls, nineteen in all, waited with the two teachers along the school's rear driveway. "Call Schlueter. Done with his deliveries, he might could drive you and the teams to Arlington. Even with a jump, that darned bus won't start."

Freddie was worried, since it was to be the last baseball meeting of the year with our archrival, and we had scores to settle. "Gosh," he suggested to Coach as he followed the older man into the aged brick building, "maybe we should call some of our mothers to caravan us to Arlington."

"He hates driving us," Astrid said, giving old Ray the evil eye. "I bet there's not a damn thing wrong with the bus."

"Just settle down, girls," came Miss Ramsell's quiet, stern voice. "Kismet will prevail."

Lo and behold, kismet did. Most of us were amazed that Schlueter got there as fast as his old beer truck could bring him. No one was prepared for the sight that met us when the teachers closed us inside the dark, chilly truck and went to sit in the September-warm cab. Only sealed cases of cold cans were stacked in the center, but we immediately littered the floorboards with hastily ripped cardboard. Probably, Schlueter should not have left the beer and, surely, not the stack of shiny, steel church keys.

Quickly, the prairie hour passed, and the pile of empty cans grew. Robbie and Freddie drank the most of all the boys, but Astrid and I were the only girls who had any at all. Still, we made up for the others; it seemed we both had hollow legs, and anything and everyone was soon hilarious.

Trying to look sober didn't work for the boys, as Sandy Shaefer threw just three balls about ten feet from the plate, and Robbie threw up vehemently in the outfield. "Under forfeit," the umpire declared as he stopped the game and none-too-gently assisted our laughing catcher, Freddie, to his feet. Vomit still spewed in center field, and Coach was taking purposeful strides toward his green-gilled outfielder as the girls' game began on the other diamond.

Where had my fastball gone? X-ray vision, for which Miss Ramsell was famous, spotted the two heavy cans in my warm-up jacket on the bench. "You get out, now," she screeched and made arm motions to our only other softball pitcher.

Zonked, giggling, and unable to find the mound, Astrid sank onto the grass, and we took both forfeits, the stuff of which kismet and small-town legends are made.

IN THE SEAT OF IDOLS

I LONGED TO BE A LADY. LADIES WERE PERFUMED. THEIR HEMS were even; they had white hands and wore hats. My mama smelled nice, but her hands were dirty from the garden in summer or chalky gray in winter from the residue of the clay she sculpted at the dining room table. Her only hat was not an ornament, but ragged straw to keep the sun from her tender skin, and she cried a lot when she thought no one knew. I was sure that real ladies didn't cry. The other women in my life, aunts on farms near our little hamlet of three hundred souls, were callused and loud. Their arms and necks were permanently brown from the sun, and I didn't know they owned dresses until Grandma's funeral.

Mrs. Habberstad was the banker's wife, and the first lady I tried to emulate as a young teen. I passed her house at least twice a day as I walked to and from school and dawdled to catch sight of her bringing in the morning milk or the afternoon paper. Her blonde hair was always in place, and her skin was clear and smooth. She wore glasses, and on her they looked wonderful. Her little, blonde daughter was well-behaved and quiet in school and always responded immediately when her mother called gently from their front porch. When Mrs. Habberstad was downtown, she nodded to everyone.

I bemoaned my dark hair, glasses, blotched skin, propensity to clown, my awkwardness around others. So I bought acne potions and Evening in Paris with the little money I scraped together and tried not to cry at the sad parts in the books I read or when my rowdy baby brother cuddled up and said he loved me. When I remembered, I modulated my voice to the sweet tinkle of my idol's. She had only spoken to me once, and that was to scold me for taking a lilac from the enormous bush that hung over the sidewalk in her front yard. "Don't steal, not even a lilac for your mother," she told me then, though she wasn't angry.

I was a girl who wanted to be just like Mrs. Habberstad, someone whose real life I never knew. But I grew up and married and moved away, and still I was not a lady. No matter what city I lived in, I fixated on women I'd like to be, but the beast within didn't change. I reveled in books—not self-help books or anything ladylike, but those of Hemingway and Michener, Ayn Rand and Robert Heinlein. My hair always needed combing or trimming and looked ridiculous beneath the pricey hats I bought often and seldom wore. I yelled at my children and wept at the Little Big Horn Battlefield and Appomattox Courthouse. I did learn to nod and acquiesce in conversations with other women; too many times, I had mistaken ladylike politeness for genuine interest and waxed verbose on some subject or another until I noticed the glazed look in their eyes. *Egg on my face again,* I'd think, and vow once more never to speak of anything more stirring than the weather or the price of hamburger. In yet another city, in my mid-thirties, I spied the woman who changed my life: my last idol.

Many ladies played bridge. I am certain that is why I went to the bridge center, enrolled in beginner's lessons, and became a whiz at the game almost immediately. Soon, I graduated to duplicate games held there. I played in a foursome with her on one Saturday afternoon.

She was blonde, serene, and soft-spoken—an attorney's wife, so reminiscent of Mrs. Habberstad. Fifteen years earlier, she'd have worn a hat to the session, I was certain. Her purse always matched her shoes, and she didn't nitpick and rail at her partner's mistakes or her opponents' victories. I was already uncomfortable at the raw and unkind gibes these duplicate bridge players bestowed on one another and wondered if the enjoyment of the game was worth enduring them. This woman's attitude was a pool of refreshing water in which to plunge my agitation. I used her as a touchstone, locating her countenance across the room. I didn't talk to her, of course. Cats and queens, you know.

She played always on Tuesdays and Saturdays, and I went to the games at those times. Once, in the months I watched and wanted to be her, I was involved in conversation at her table. While we waited for others to finish their play so we could move on to our next tables, one of the women commented on my idol's complexion. She told a sweet story about her mother's insistence that she cream her face before she went to bed at night, no matter what the time. She ended with a little giggle, after telling of getting in at all hours during college years and hearing the tape of her mother's voice in her brain: *Cream your face. Cream your face.* I was enthralled, forgot myself and engaged my mouth before I put my brain in gear.

"Tough luck for me," I clowned, patting my ample hip. "The only tape my mother left me was 'Clean your plate.'"

They laughed, of course, even as my face burned, and I wondered if I'd ever learn. I'd been an unladylike fool in front of this woman I so admired. I decided to skip the Saturday night game.

They were remodeling the bridge center, so the club played in the basement of an antiquated office building for a few weeks. I stood in front of its one, tiny woman's bathroom, fidgeting since I had waited until the last minute again. My idol emerged. I babbled an inane greeting, rushed inside to the single stall and plopped down on her still-warm urine.

Her mother left her at least two tapes, my mind roared as I scrubbed myself and the toilet seat. *'Don't ever sit on public toilet seats' was the second one!*

I am a new woman since that night: the same old girl with a fresh understanding, empowered with the acceptance of who I am and what I am not. In my life now are many women, some like me and many who are not, but none whom I envy. I have the lady whose name I never knew to thank for that.

Thanks, Lady.

SETKA

1952, AND THE WORLD WAS AT A POLICE ACTION. MY YOUNG Marine sergeant husband would undoubtedly be in the next shipment out to Korea from the Naval Air Station here on Coronado Island, California. I was sixteen, a little bit pregnant, and excited. My Aunt Lois's letter promised a box of Christmas goodies.

So Christmas would come to the land of perennial sunshine and three-foot geraniums, after all. It would arrive in the form of setka, the traditional Danish holiday loaf that sealed Aunt Lois's fame as the family baker each year. I was glad to be away from the South Dakota prairie snowdrifts, but couldn't imagine Christmas without setka. I raved and paced, sang its praises and anticipated.

The package finally came. Divinity, fudge, cookies, fruitcake, even a potholder. Largess surrounded the wax-wrapped prize. I snatched it up, buttered and gobbled the heel of the loaf, then thin-sliced two pieces to toast under the gas broiler for my husband's supper. I served them up with a flourish and a vocal trumpet blast. Ta rum da DUM da da!

He crunched the proffered delicacy with appropriate reverence. I watched breathlessly as each brown-dotted, pale morsel, the merest hint of heavenly icing on one end, disappeared. At last he spoke.

"This is raisin bread."

ADD THE LOVE

I STOLE MY FIRST COOKBOOK. IT WAS IN A BARREL IN THE STORAGE room next to the dank basement apartment we rented from Eda B. Merritt on Marietta Drive, and I was a desperate, sixteen-year old bride.

"Well, old boy, can she cook?" The marines stationed at the Naval Air Station on Coronado Island had only one question for their young supply sergeant, my new husband. He had been motherless for years and didn't have that home cooking comparison. But his answer, always the same, wasn't a joke. He meant it.

"Well, guys, she cooks. But it ain't like the mess hall."

I needed to cook at least as well as the mess hall, and fast.

The purloined sixth edition, completely revised, of Fannie Merritt Farmer's Boston Cooking-School Cook Book was a 1937 printing, first published in 1896. It was a sturdy, hardcover book, already yellowed with age. The first page advertised Magic Covers that prevented dough from sticking to breadboards and rolling pins (I had neither), and the company would send one postpaid from Newport, Maine for a dollar. Dollars were hard to come by during the Korean

War, but I coveted a Magic Cover. Somehow, I knew my dough was going to stick, and I should be prepared.

I skipped over the chapters dedicated to menu planning, equipment, and methods. I just wanted to know how to make the things my mother cooked: pork roasts, meat loaf, escalloped potatoes, and homemade yeast rolls that pulled apart into three pieces and tantalized you with their odor while they were baking.

And gravy. My bridegroom wanted gravy. Page 196 showed me how to do it. Page 89 was a lifesaver, in those days before Bisquick; baking powder biscuits were time-consuming with only a mesh strainer for a flour sifter, but otherwise easy to create. A fried hamburger patty, green peas from a can, biscuits and gravy, and ice cream for dessert was my first real meal. It garnered raves of approval and sent me off and running about the business of cooking. Dreams of writing the Great American Novel went on hold while acquiring pots, pans, and potato ricers became an obsession, concocting perfect dishes my ultimate goal. Adding the love was to come many years, many tears later.

In the intervening half century plus, Mrs. Merritt's cookbook has become tattered and fragile. In the '90s, my daughter scored me a 1959 Bantam paperback edition at a garage sale for a dime. I use it as reference to make the staples that now add the love in my kitchen: homemade mayonnaise, Cleveland and Bleu Cheese dressings, huckleberry jams and syrups, rhubarb-fig marmalade, bread pudding, and cooked-in-water custard pie.

The original book, held together with twine, occupies a place of honor in the cupboard in our family room. I open it a couple of times a year, remember Mrs. Merritt, and am sorry I don't know whether her late husband was related to Fanny Merritt Farmer. I ponder whether she ever knew of my theft, and wonder about an afterlife in which she knows I finally wanted to 'fess up and make amends, but it was too late.

Before I put it away, I always read Fanny Farmer's preface to her first edition of this book that has been a companion piece to my life. It begins: "But for life, the universe were nothing; and all that has life requires nourishment." And I rejoice in my confirmed, recent years' perception that nourishment wears many disguises. Whether it's cordon bleu or a delivered pizza, an attaboy or a necessary scolding, I must not forget to add the love.

MEMORIES OF A CAR TRIP

I AM PACKING FOR THIS TRIP TO NEW YORK CITY, TAKEN hard on the heels of a quick journey to Los Angeles, and am still troubled by my Southern California visit. While there, I asked my old friend about the unparalleled Mexican restaurant we used to visit across the boulevard and deep in old Los Nietos. Was it still there? Was it possible the old woman still cooked? Could we eat there tonight? My trip to Southern California after a thirty-year absence was brief, and my time with her would be only that evening. I thought perhaps I could kill the proverbial two birds by gorging on both Mamacita's enchiladas and many years of gossip and shared remembrances over dinner.

My friend's face actually fell, unsupported for a moment by political correctness. She quickly replaced it with the familiar, serene mask. "Oh, we haven't been there for years," she replied brightly, and went on only at my insistence. "Well, the Pachuco gangs took over the streets there years ago, Judith. And now, well, people just tend to stay with their own, you know." The words came haltingly toward the end of her explanation and compelled me to look up from the photograph album in my lap. Fear lurked just behind her eyes.

She's afraid, I thought. *Scared to go where we took the kids on Sunday afternoons not all that long ago.*

How sad, how terminally sad, I continued to muse as I picked at ersatz Mexican cuisine in an upscale Montebello eatery while we caught up on the years gone by. *Some things just can't be revisited, I guess. And I have such sweet memories of Los Nietos.*

Therefore, I am thinking a lot about my first real trip to New York City as I prepare for this next visit to the Big Apple, forty-five years later. What will the differences be, and can they break my heart? The World Trade Center will not dominate the Manhattan skyline and, though I never saw the twin towers, I am certain to experience renewed anguish at their absence. I am traveling alone and thus will have quiet time to contain my rage at mankind's lunacy, evidenced so purely by the evil of September 11. And I am flying in and out. That is surely different, for the other was a car trip.

And what a car! A Cadillac four-door limousine convertible with side mounts and body by Fisher, this car was one of only six built and three in existence and nearly always stopped traffic wherever it traveled. Only eighteen years old on that early summer journey in 1958 from Iowa to a Buck Hills Falls, Pennsylvania car show, it was nonetheless a charter member of the Classic Car Club of America. It sported thirteen coats of gleaming hand-rubbed black lacquer, an awesome length of pure white canvas top, elegant hunter green leather seats, and a rear interior big enough to house the crib for our happy, golden girl, nine-month old Dorcas Leigh. We were taking her to stay with her grandparents in Washington, D.C. before we went to the classic car gathering.

Sometimes, Dorcas played all night and slept in the mornings, and it had been one of those nights when we found our threesome alone at 11 a.m. in the breakfast room of a pricey turnpike hotel. Our breakfast was ordered but not yet served when an ebullient, snappy dresser and his elegant wife came in and took a table nearby. My, he looked familiar. They both nodded and smiled, and I was a little uneasy. How did I know him? The waitress took the couple's order and hadn't been out of sight a minute when the guy was surrounded by kitchen help, all brandishing menus and pieces of paper, thrusting pens into his space. "Mr. Thomas, what an honor! Will you sign this for me, please?"

Of course. He was Danny Thomas, the television star. I didn't watch much except baseball and had never seen his show, but his schnozz was unmistakable. She was Rosemary, his wife of many years. I had read about their atypical celebrity marriage somewhere.

Our breakfast came, and I determined not to intrude. He had no such restraint. Enchanted by our baby's curly hair and the gusto with which she smacked at toast and scrambled egg, Danny Thomas glided over to stand beside her high chair and place his index finger lightly on her button nose.

"Call that a nose, baby girl? Looks like an inverted wart to me!"

His laughter was infectious, and the four of us were soon engaged in conversation between mouthfuls. They had driven all the way from Los Angeles to Atlantic City to do a benefit for his pet charity, Saint Jude's Children's Hospital, and were

on their way home. I was impressed, not so much with his
fame but with his dedication to that cause. I also thought he
was funny—the wart joke, ad lib, was sidesplitting. We left
the restaurant together, and he asked a favor. "May I take a
picture of your car?" We each took a picture, and drove off
in different directions.

Alone, we went to New York City after the car show.
A woman who worked for my husband for many years now
lived in Larchmont, a New York bedroom community, and
he wanted to surprise her with a visit. After a few short hours
in the fabulous city where I had never been except to a game
at Yankee Stadium when I was a teenager, we got on the
road to Larchmont. Yeah, sure.

It is reported that all men are this way: they simply will
not ask for directions. Jokes with this theme have amused
Homo sapiens for years, probably centuries. "Why are there
millions of sperm for each little ovum?" "Because they won't
get directions for the trip!" You've heard them all, I know,
but in my husband's case, it was so true as to be unfunny.
He soon took a wrong exit, and we were rolling slowly on
a narrow, crowded street with tall, faded brick apartment
buildings on both sides. Dilapidated vehicles lined the weed-
cracked sidewalks.

"It's just like 'A Tree Grows in Brooklyn,'" I said. "Look
at the fire escapes and the plants on them, the laundry
on those short little lines." I had lived in two major cities
already, but this kind of neighborhood had hitherto existed
only in the novels I devoured. As I inhaled the atmosphere,
I realized that all the folks on the sidewalks and the fire
escapes were Negroes. We were probably in Harlem, and the
car was attracting a lot of attention.

They came from nowhere and everywhere. Mostly boys—five-footers, six-footers, and a few so high above the group that I knew they were taller than George Mikan, my Minnesota Lakers basketball hero. They flooded the street around the car on all sides and filled the summer air with their uproar. "What is it? Where'd you get it? Where you going?" We couldn't move through the crowd, so Albert shut off the engine.

He was more protective of that car than he was of his family, I often complained, so he noticed immediately that the boys were not touching it. They were examining it closely, reverently, from the rear bumper to the hood ornament, their bodies circling slowly around it, the group moving with one accord. Relieved, Albert gestured through the driver's window, and a space formed for him to open the door and step into the crowd. How incongruous he was, foreign in his pale skin and gray suit and tie, surrounded by gleaming black youths in motley array. He held up his hands for silence, and it came with a bang, the absence of their yells suddenly deafening.

"I'm lost," he admitted. "If someone will give me directions back to the thruway that goes to Larchmont, I'll tell you all about it. Even show you the works."

They chattered again, decibels lower than their earlier clamor, and five or six boys extricated themselves and ran at top speed down the street to a barbershop. Albert, doing what he loved best, was already pointing and talking to his rapt audience when the boys returned with an older man who knew the way we wanted to go.

It grew by osmosis, the sea of dark faces, now joined on the fringes by neighborhood adults of both sexes, all listening intently to my husband's discourse on the provenance of his classic car. Soon there were hundreds milling quietly, attempting to get a peek when he took off his jacket and tossed it into the front seat, rolled up his white sleeves and lifted the hood to display the "works." I was afraid we were never going to be able to move down the street as ten, fifteen, then twenty minutes passed while the black maelstrom swirled, each wave taking its split second turn to view the spotless black and chrome engine.

It had to end. My husband finally turned his back to the car and spoke to the people. "Thanks for the directions, gang, and for liking my car. We really have to go, now, okay?" There were young murmurs of disappointment as he closed and locked the hood, but a space cleared for his return to the car.

I have traveled to many places and seen a myriad of splendid things, but there are few memories that still raise gooseflesh on my forearms as this one does: The black sea parted. It split in two immediately and without an errant ripple. It lined the street with two feet to spare on either side of the car, uniformly and without a sound, and waved us out of sight. I watched through the rear window until I could no longer see its smiles and waves.

That autumn, I tuned in to the season premiere of "The Danny Thomas Show." The familiar face looked quizzically at the audience as he stood, center stage, and began his monologue. "You call those noses out there? They look like inverted warts to me!" I suppose the joke was already written, the program already taped, before he left for Atlantic City. Nevertheless, I want to believe, to remember, that the little joke he made for Dorcas Leigh became part of his next show.

Now, this week, I am going again to New York. I will see the Metropolitan Museum of Art, and bask in Van Gogh, Degas, and Monet until I am bursting with joy. I'll buy a hot pretzel and ride the subway to Battery and the Staten Island Ferry. But I don't think I'll go to Harlem. My memories are too sweet.

SILVER HAWK

Part One

MY HOUSEWIFE CAR WAS A FOUR-YEAR-OLD COMMANDER.
Boring. It was the dullest of banal Mr. Studebaker's auto-
mobiles and even out-humdrummed Nash's Ramblers for
unappealing. Just as every Rambler wagon on the road was
a glaring, two-tone green, my pointy sedan with the wraparound rear window was peachy beige with a maroon top
and twin to every sixth car on the suburban streets. I wanted
a Golden Hawk.

He didn't refuse me many things, but the Hawk dia-
logue remained closed. The boss's wife drove a wraparound
Commander, maroon and beige, and that was that. He re-
ferred to the '37 Cord he was restoring, the coffin-nosed
monstrosity whose dead body and appurtenances used all but
lawnmower room in the attached garage of our California
cul-de-sac home.

"It's going to be for you, honey, and it's twenty times
classier than any old Golden Hawk. Plus, it was thirty years
ahead of its time, anyway, with the front wheel drive and all.
It won't be long," he promised. He'd been working on it for

four years; in another four it would be thirty years old and, by his own admitted timeframe, mediocre. I didn't want to wait.

I won't say the Studebaker controversy was the reason I divorced him; it actually was about his not knowing—no, not caring—how many teams competed in the World Series. But when I found myself alone with a loose eight hundred dollars, a veritable fortune in my eyes, I left the three little kids with a neighbor and went car shopping.

There it was! On a used car lot on Rosemead Boulevard sat a '57 Hawk, its grill, sleek fins, and chrome striping reminiscent of the science fiction that had influenced my life since I discovered H.G. Wells at the age of eight. I was already past the entrance and had to drive what seemed forever to turn around and make a dangerous dash across the busy thoroughfare. The little Commander slunk into a parking space beside the office trailer and sat there quietly, apologetic, surely aware that the pink slip in the tiny glove box meant it wouldn't be going home with me. I swung my Jane Russell body up the rough wood steps to outsell the salesman.

"There's a pink Golden Hawk on the far corner," I flirted. "How much is it?"

He was the classic used car salesman, right down to his graying, gypsy good looks and outlandish sport coat. He wore a wedding ring, however, and didn't seem very flirtatious. I toned it down a bit. Childlike now, I continued.

"I don't have much to spend, but I've always wanted one. Can I go sit in it?"

He was down the steps in a flash and replied only when he took my hand to help me navigate the rough boards. "It's actually a Silver, but a beauty—'57, and a great price."

I pretended to be returning to the Commander. "Come on," he beseeched. "When you sit in it you won't know you're not in a Golden. Give it a try, eh?"

I allowed him to persuade me. Playing reluctant, I sat amid the pale pink leather of the car built to be mine. I bemoaned the fact that it was automatic transmission, not mentioning that the last stick I'd driven was my folks' '38 Chevy with 4 on the floor or that the despised Commander trade-in was also automatic. I complained about a tiny cigarette burn and the stale odor of smoke (I burned up three packs of 29¢ filters a day, myself) and about the coupe's 87,000 miles. I allowed him to persuade me that all used cars were sold 'As Is,' without warranty, and I didn't even test-drive it. After I haggled the price down as far as I could, I signed over the Commander and parted with $750. The Hawk and I left the lot, and I didn't whoop for joy until we were out of the salesman's sight.

It was less than three miles to my house, but I had already stopped whooping. Steam obscured my vision, and the hood looked like it was going to pop off and fly back to its home planet. The neighbor's husband was home from his day shift at the nearest aircraft plant, and he shook his head. "No warranty? As is, huh? Well, the water pump is shot on this baby, and I'll bet it costs plenty to replace it."

We decided the best thing for me to do was drive it back immediately and see if the salesman wouldn't do the right thing by me. To that end, the neighbor filled some water jugs and set them on the floorboard on the passenger's side with instructions to replace water every few blocks, "…before the gauge gets in the red," between home and the car lot.

I added fuel to the plan and collected my children from his back yard. Chubby little girl was wet and filthy, as only a three-year-old can get on a Slip 'n' Slide, and cranky from going without her nap. The boys were five and seven and also grubby, and I delighted in the large hole in the shoulder of Dougie's tee shirt. I piled them prominently in the coupe's small rear seat and wended my burnt-fingered way back to Rosemead, rehearsing a poor-young-mother plea as I drove. The gauge was edging toward the red again by the time I drove into the lot and parked next to the Commander. Its wraparound rear now resembled a gleeful sneer.

Mr. Salesman came down the steps. I looked sorrowful, gestured at the car full of urchins, choked back tears and began. "I barely got it home. The water pump...What will I do?...I can't afford..."

His expression didn't change, and he was not unkind, but he yawned scorn with every word when he interrupted my scene. "I'll get you a new water pump, ma'am. No charge. And I would always have gotten you a new water pump. You can come back for the Hawk on Friday noon." He was up and down the steps and handing me the keys to the Commander when he spoke his last words.

"But I want you to know, ma'am, that I think you're about as helpless as a cobra."

Part Two

THE HAWK AND I DECLINED AT ABOUT THE SAME PACE. THE divorce judge allowed me a payment-free four years in the family home, to finish my degree and begin a career. It seemed like forever, right up to the degreeless day I came home from shopping and drinking and couldn't get into the driveway because a moving truck was in the way. Ex-husband was there directing the job. He said I'd had ninety days' notice that the home was sold. I didn't remember. He took the children for the weekend, and I followed the van to a new home, a tract house he'd rented in my name just a few blocks away.

There the Hawk had to sit on the street, where the birds that resided in the orange trees added insult to its unbathed body's injuries. Scratches and dings on its fair chassis told the story of drunken parking and more, and the left headlight frame was suspiciously bent. I drove it to my rather responsible job nearly every day, too seldom to classes at night, and far too often to the Serene Room with its dim lights, piano bar, and few hours of escape from the unnamed terror that stalked my spirit.

It clamored against my neglect, the lovely Silver Hawk. It first failed its brakes in heavy go-to-work traffic, days after I let the insurance lapse. I'd barely dug myself out of that financial hole when it dropped its reverse gear without warning. Straight-ahead driving, no mean trick, worked for a couple of months until one day the "Drive" gear shuddered at me one last time before the coupe finally jerked forward. I bemoaned my automobile fate over Black Jack Daniel's and beer at the bar that night.

"I don't even know for sure if I can exit the parking lot," I complained. "Even though I'm parked to drive straight out."

"No Studebaker is worth a nickel," my favorite bartender chided me. "Seriously, that Hawk ain't worth a hundred bucks." I liked him, but I was incensed at the slight.

A would-be friend approached me before the night was over. He had a Monza I could have, he said, if I could buy one tire and pay for the title transfer. It wasn't worth the powder to blow it, either, he indicated, but it was running. He followed me home "to see where I lived," and brought the car the next afternoon.

The Silver Hawk sat in the gutter under the orange trees in the weeks that followed. It grew more dusty and speckled, until a front tire was flat and the neighbors complained. "I'll sell it," I told them, and put an ad in the Friday Nickel. Saturday morning the phone rang early.

"Does it run?" The young man's voice was excited.

"Yes, it runs, but there's no reverse gear and a front tire is flat."

"I'll be right there. Don't sell it to anyone else."

He brought a check and his last bank statement to prove that his check was good and showed me his drivers' license. After I'd signed the title, he went out and started the engine.

"I'll be back with a tire tomorrow," he said. "I'm sure I can drive it away. You know, ma'am, now that it's mine, I want to tell you that you sold it far too cheap." He wasn't gloating; it was more like shame.

I pooh–poohed him. "No, no, that's all I wanted," I argued. "Have a good time with it."

I got in the Monza when he left, to go shopping and drinking. I couldn't wait to get to the Serene Room with the last word: to show my no-longer-favorite bartender the check for $125.00.

Part Three

It is nearly two generations later as I recall these events and consign them to the printed page. They came to the forefront of my memory during Washington State's recent giant lottery. It rose to an unheard-of twenty-seven million dollars, and people who never indulged were standing in lines to buy lottery tickets. My two lady friends and I went to the local mini-mart and stood in a line. Clutching our tickets on the way home, one of them began to tell what she would do with the jackpot. When the second woman was through recounting all the good things the lottery would afford her, they turned to me. "What would you do with it, Judith?"

I hadn't thought, but I didn't hesitate. "I don't know what else," I answered, "but I'd spend a bunch of it on a '57 Studebaker Silver Hawk. Preferably a pink one."

AMERICAN PATCH

The author says:
    Half my life was behind me when I came to a bare realization of the "ripple effect" we homo sapiens have on one another—how a smile here can save a stranger a tongue-lashing down the road, and how growth-challenged (read: immature!) persons like me can charge through the countryside of our lives virtually unaware of the existence of others. I was already actively correcting this basic character flaw in myself when the instance of the American Patch occurred. It caused me to stop, look, and pray that the next half of my life would be long enough to make amends for the first.

I WAS MY MOTHER'S HOUSE-SLAVE: CHATTEL PROPAGATED FOR the express purpose of freedom to sculpt her hair and nails and the wet clay or papier-mâché that dominated our dining room table. At seven and eight years old, I dusted and daily swept the wood and linoleum floors of our rented wartime houses, my short-handled broom often leaving splinters if I gripped too close to the sawn-off part. By the time I was nine, I could rinse a brush-scrubbed floor and wax it better than any housewife, and it was a routine part of my "Saturday work." By age ten, I was doing the laundry every Sunday during the school year, and on regular Washday Monday during summer vacation. Mama was particular about "the wash," as she called it.

In the basement of the house I lived in from 1947 until I escaped the South Dakota prairie in 1952 stood the dour Maytag washer and the separate, wobbly, roll-about rinse tubs. Three rinses were mandatory, and she had better not catch me stinting. I washed the whites, then the coloreds, then the darks in the same water, wringing them all into empty wicker baskets. When the soupy, gray water was drained from the machine I filled it again, and the wet clothes sloshed around in the first rinse water in that order. Then they were wrung into the rinse tubs, the last one laced with Mrs. Stewart's Bluing. There I swished them up and down by hand.

The Maytag's hard rubber wringer was electric and had a mind of its own. Have you heard the expression "tit in a wringer?" It's not so funny when you've lived it. But I digress.

She was particular, and I hated her. I despised her beauty and her indolence and her nitpicking, and I hung a perfect wash in order to escape her tongue. In minus 25° weather— not uncommon in Eastern Dakota in those years—she still insisted that the white wash be hung on the outdoor clotheslines before I went to school. "Freezing whitens the bedding and underwear," she swore. I unpinned a thousand tons of stiff-as-a-board sheets and tee shirts on the dark winter Monday afternoons of my youth. I manhandled them awkwardly down steep wooden steps, careful not to break them, just to unfreeze and dry them gray-white on the lines in the basement. There they joined the colored clothes, Father's work clothes, us girls' couple of dresses and Little Brother's jeans.

She added the ironing to my chores in seventh grade, and the mending the summer I graduated from the eighth. Raised during the Great Depression as she was, nothing was discarded if it could be darned or patched. Little Brother routinely tore out the knees of his jeans, and Father's work shirts had many three-cornered tears from being caught on the spikes of the electric poles he climbed. The mending basket was full when she sat down with me that summer Tuesday.

"Mend before you do the ironing each week," she instructed. "That way you can press out the patches when the iron is cooling." She showed me how to darn Father's work socks with the big needle and the soft darning thread: "Loose, now, so it won't bunch up when it shrinks in its first wash." I had a vivid picture of the whack I'd get if Father's foot got blistered from my bunched-up darning, so I paid close attention. Her pale fingers, so adroit at carving and sculpting and piano playing, flew in and out as she demonstrated the techniques to be used. She issued a benign giggle at my left-handed clumsiness, and I felt a cautious love for her.

I cannot forget that day: the cedar chest on which we sat side by side, her scent as she bent to show me how to match the fabric and tack it under a 3-corner rip, her insistence that I use a thimble when making the invisible stitching around the patch. My senses still record the warmth in my chest and the damp at the corner of my eyes as our shoulders touched, and I basked in the feel of her. I cannot forget the day because it was the last time I was ever lulled into la-la land by any hint of togetherness. Too soon, unhappy with my patchwork, she shrieked, ripped it out, and set me to the task again.

I became a perfect mender. Dry-eyed, silent, perfect. Sublimely soft, darned socks and flawlessly patched shirts and jeans adorned my family until the summer of '52.

Barely sixteen, I married a young farm boy turned Marine who was probably destined for tragic death on a frozen Korean wasteland. He could care less about washing and patching but wished wholeheartedly that my mother had taught me some culinary skills. I had as little experience with cohabitation as I did with cooking—in the dysfunctional home where I was raised, we lived together on separate planets—and none with love. My childish demands and search for perfection made me a less-than-perfect wife. He didn't go to Korea, and I took our child and left him alone in stark government housing without a backward glance.

It was, however, an era when a woman's ideal was husband, house, and 2.8 children, so I married again at nineteen. He was older and well-to-do. He adored me, and I tried desperately to keep my feet on the conjugal planet. But suburbia, an automatic washer, and conversations about the crabgrass battle grew stale, and part-time jobs and part-time school did not fill the perfection void. I took my jewelry and 3.0 children and left the pleasant California cul-de-sac without a second thought.

"Why?" he asked at divorce court.

"Because," I answered. Because. It was enough reason for me and my loveless heart.

Milt was different, as was the wild ride of the next marriage. He was 43 to my 28 when we flew to Vegas on a whim and found time to tie the knot between piles of chips and bottles of champagne. He was a blue-collar working man who trained Labrador Retrievers, hunted birds in the Imperial Valley, and epitomized America and Apple Pie.

"I'm gonna be sorry I did this," he said, as he stooped to kiss his bride in the gaudy chapel. "But, oh, I love you so."

He did, I know, and I had a hitherto unknown feeling for him. Unlike any other man he confronted me and, unlike any other of my marital relationships, I did not ignore him. I didn't treat him well, of course, but I was uncomfortably aware of his presence in my life. I screamed, cursed, threw things.

"What is really the matter with you right now," he'd demand when we were arguing. "How can (whatever the topic was) be so important as to turn you into a shrieking witch?"

I'd yell louder, break something important, and he'd ultimately go to his sister's for days or weeks. Our good times—taking the boys to dog trials, valet-parking his battered pickup while we lunched at the Brown Derby, drinking French Seventy-Fives at the Serene Room's piano bar, the single bed where a sweet dawn would find our two long bodies nestled like spoons—kept us together for nearly three years.

It was during a good time that Milt was ecstatic one day. He'd scored two—count 'em, two!—American-made work shirts in his size at a closeout store. "Probably the last two in the whole U.S. of A.," he griped as he took them from the battered sack to show me. They were long-sleeved in the shaved flannel he preferred, with intricate, colored stripes on a background of light gray and pale green. Perhaps I was glad for him and his find, but what I remember is only an intellectual curiosity about his American-made obsession.

He tore the sleeve on the new gray shirt the first day it was worn. It was a small, three-cornered rent and too high on the arm to roll the sleeves over it. You'd think he'd lost a child, or at least a puppy, the way he carried on. He tossed it with disgust to the bottom of the closet, and it lay there until the weekend. He was working overtime, and I was doing the working woman's Saturday chores when I picked it up.

There was plenty of material inside the placket to rob a piece for patchwork. "It's a huge challenge," I mused. "That pattern is very small and structured, hard to match. But I'll bet I can still put a perfect patch on it."

I ran to the dime store for pale gray thread and sat in the good living room light to tackle the job. I had not lost my touch. As I pressed the new patch with a cooling iron, the rip and its stitches were rendered invisible. Perfect again, I thought and, filled with pride, hung it on his side of the closet and went to firmly inspect the kids' Saturday work.

It was days later when he came from the bedroom with the shirt in his hands and a bemused look of adoration on his face. "Honey, this is so beautiful. Oh, sweetheart, what a nice surprise."

I don't know what I responded. I'd moved on since the patch challenge was conquered, and it didn't have anything to do with him, anyway. I heard him showing it to his hunting partner, though, as they left for a weekend. "Look at this. Can't even see it. Judith did it for me." I was proud that he was proud—you know what I mean?

Our final bad time arrived. He was gone, and I was throwing his stuff methodically onto the cement slab in back when I spied his favorite shotgun standing up in the corner of the closet. I'd seen him bragging about it and the added cost of its hand-carved stock alone. I took it by the barrels and pounded it against a steel corner post in the front yard until it lay in parts and splinters.

His voice was hoarse with emotion when he collected his things. "Even you would not do this, Judith," he said, and he gathered the pieces of the shotgun and left me for the last time. I missed him, once in a while.

A generation passed; my progeny escaped and created house-slaves or scapegoats or beloved children of their own. Life crises afforded me late maturity and the seedlings of insight into myself and the world in which I had to learn to participate if I would live. Little Brother declined to participate and died a violent death before his thirtieth birthday. Mama was gone soon after, and Sister and I discovered we had not one shared memory from all the years we lived together. I spent an increasing amount of time in introspection and was just beginning to recognize the enormity of my early disregard for others when Milt came to my city on a train.

He was visiting World War II army buddies across the continent on an Amtrak pass. One of those pals lived here, and he called my daughter from the hotel. "We're the only kids he ever had, Mom," she chided me. "I'm having him to dinner, and you're going to the Red Lion to pick him up."

He was sixty-six and nearly blind, his lean Texan's body fattened to bursting, yet the years disappeared when he spoke. "You're still purtier than a speckled pup," he drawled when I stepped into his room, and soon we were chatting like old friends, just like in the best of our good times, only better. He told me about his wife and their fine life; I spoke of my work, my children, and their children.

"No jewelry," he noted and pointed to my hands. "What ever happened to that big diamond of yours?" I told him the pat and comical story of how I sold it for a song to get out of L.A., and how I'd never looked back.

"Remember that Tiger Eye you gave me, Judith? My hands got too fat for it, and my wife prefers I just wear my wedding ring, anyway. Remember it? It's in that jewel box there." He gestured at a small leather case on the dresser next to me. I lifted the lid.

Was I supposed to notice it, the cloth that enclosed the ring? I tried to read his eyes behind their coke-bottle lenses, but his demeanor didn't change, and he went on with his friendly chatter. Great shame rose and threatened to spill from my throat. I turned my head to blink away moisture. Then I took the ring from the box. Its 20-year-old wrapping humbled my existence.

"Yep, that's it!" I forced gaiety as I held them in the palm of my hand. "Shall we go to that girl's for dinner now?"

He stood and rummaged for his key card while I replaced the Tiger Eye in the center section of the jewel box. Its two-inch square wrapper of striped, pale gray flannel was the last thing I saw as I dropped the lid, the perfect three-corner patch in the center surely a symbol of something.

PANTHER, RESTING

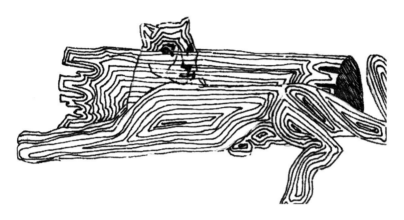

SHE WOULD SEE HIM A COUPLE OF NIGHTS A WEEK AT THE first of her prescribed watering holes, the uptown bistro where she drank cognac with a coke back and handed out her real name on the rare occasion anyone asked. She didn't know his name, even if she'd ever heard Frank or another customer call it, and his neat presence didn't disrupt her narrowing world in their early near-encounters. Seated on a high stool there at the circular piano bar, he seemed a small man, perhaps fifteen years older than her twenty-eight, always in a dark suit and necktie and never intoxicated. However, once he had imbibed several drinks, Frank, the resident keyboard artist, could coax him to sing a show tune or two in an indecisive baritone. She dismissed him as she dismissed the bulk of the planet's occupants; he offered her nothing and didn't sing very well.

At first, Frank often asked her to sing alone. He liked her voice when she sang along with the crowd, but she knew she was no Patrice Munsel and had a quarter century's practice in avoiding activities at which she did not excel. She kept

going back because she liked his expertise at the piano and
the polite ambiance of his bar; few men attempted to pick
her up, those that did were genteel when rebuffed, and
Frank finally stopped asking her to vocalize. Her work, the
children waiting at home for whom she was responsible, and
her bars—this was the sum total of her existence.

After sipping two drinks in Frank's establishment, usually
as far as she got from home in the evening, she would have
two careful scotch mists without twists in the piano lounge
of a West Whittier bowling alley and finish her evening with
two sour mash bourbons, backed with ten-cent beer. The
long, dark bar near home—her 'bourbon bar'—was her last
stop, the haven where she put her day to rest. She always
arrived there by 10:30, and sometimes left with the diehards
when "Last call!" thundered at 2:00 AM. On those nights,
increasingly more frequent at the time of this story, truth
rewrote itself in those compartments of her mind to which
she relegated all chaos, and she always remembered only two
bourbons and two short beers as she drove the careful six
blocks of residential streets to her house.

About once a month, she left her bourbon bar early
and didn't go home. She drove over the hills to La Puente,
where there was an avenue of noisy nightclubs, their garish,
otherworldly neon masking the grimy despair of the
night street. There she drank anything that someone else
was buying, danced as if she enjoyed it, and hogged the
microphone at every opportunity. Dawn found her always
in the same motel, sometimes alone. But by the time she
arrived at the sunlit six blocks of tract houses, she had again
rewritten her conscious history.

His arm was withered, she assumed since birth, as he was so adept at concealing the deformity. She looked up from her cognac and took notice of it because a cloth-wrapped bundle peeked from beneath the affected armpit, and the small limb thumped on the bar when he offloaded and unwrapped the carving.

"Oh, you finally brought me a piece of your work," Frank cooed while he played something from Carousel. "Nice, nice, nice."

It's about eighteen inches of cherry, she thought. *Not stained soft pine, but rock hard, oiled, and somehow living cherry.* A wave of envy rippled her spine; covetousness enveloped her as she took in the whole of the sinuous sculpture. It seemed to breathe—its whorls and smooth curves at first only suggesting the head, the tail, a log hiding place—and then overpowered her with a feline power and perfection. An overdressed woman gestured with her stem glass; two olives rolled and threatened ice blue sequins. "What's it supposed to be?"

"It's a panther, resting." Judith didn't mean to voice her thought. Everyone at the bar turned in her direction, unused to this antisocial regular joining in the conversation. She lifted her gaze from the incredible object in front of him and met his hazel eyes briefly, for the naked emotion he transmitted repulsed her. Insecurity, longing, empathy lay there in full measure. From years of practice repelling the unknown, she sent his feelings to the walled compartments in her mind and brightly amended her comment. Now blasé and sipping regally at the dregs of her first cognac, she gestured and clowned. "Or whatever you want it to be, I suspect." She didn't look at him again, not once in the many hours they both occupied space at Frank's piano bar over the following months.

On a busy Christmas shopping night, she arrived relaxed and glowing after having stopped at George and Martha's to drink some wine. She bestowed rare smiles on the regulars and listened intently to a stranger's good tenor as he sang "Green, Green Grass of Home" over the clamor of clinking glass and murmuring voices. When applause died, Frank challenged her.

"I'll bet you don't know all the words to this one, Judith," he teased, and began an introduction to "Scarlet Ribbons." It was in B-flat, her best key, and she dived right into the heartrending lyrics she knew to perfection, following Frank's key change with ease as she sang the bridge. Noise died, drinks hung suspended in midair, and her one thought as applause began to thunder was: *I feel like a real person right now.* She smiled at the crowd, feigning humility, and accidentally caught his eye. Was he showing her empathy? She left her drink and Frank's bar in a hurry.

Over the next few weeks, she spent most of her drinking time at the bourbon bar. The pianist didn't know a complete tune and masked his ignorance by inserting risqué jokes when he couldn't finish a rendition, so she staked out a stool at the far end of the long back bar and refused to think about the entertainment she was missing at Frank's. She didn't demur when the children wanted to spend the whole of Christmas vacation with their father, and so the house was most often empty. On New Year's Eve, she was lost in a fog.

She snapped back to reality from the fog of her blackout to find herself at the wheel of her car in one of the worst of L.A.'s real, ocean fogs. Creeping along a wide street at just a few miles an hour, she had no idea where she was. *Or where I've been,* she said to herself. *Or what time it is, or how I got so drunk.* This was disconcerting, an actual conscious thought about drunkenness, and it would not fly away to its safe keep when she willed it. Then she was on top of the Whittier Downs Mall. Diffused, almost invisible colored lights glowed like a beacon at the corner of Washington and Norwalk boulevards, and self-pride reigned again. She knew where she was, just two blocks from her bourbon bar, and she wanted a drink.

It was bedlam. Every booth and stool was full, and the long expanse of worn red carpet between the front door and the bathroom writhed with loud humanity. Now that she had thought of her need to pee, that need was urgent, so she braved the bodies and made her way to the paper-littered little room. The mirror reflected tangled, teased hair and smudged black around her lifeless eyes. She edged the smudges away with spit and toilet paper and put a bright smile on her red mouth. *Hope I can get to the bar,* she thought, smiling at herself, and went to get her bourbon.

The press of bodies didn't relinquish space without a fight, and she'd wriggled only a couple of yards when a man stopped her. He placed his hands—one attached to a long arm, the other to a short arm in a wrinkled sleeve—on her shoulders. She had to look up to see his face. She had never seen him here before, he was much taller than she thought, and he was very, very drunk.

"I've been trying to figure out what you're looking for," he intoned with alcohol-induced solemnity. "Trying for many months now. Are you looking for a boy or a girl?" His eyes glittered.

She ran. Beginning to weep great, hysterical sobs and gouts of tears before she was even out of his sight, she shoved and clawed her way to the exit and the safety of her Silver Hawk. Her head was a maelstrom of noise, and she laid it on the steering wheel and clamped her hands over her ears. Subdued but still weeping, Judith let the car find its way home, where she cried herself to sleep like a lost child.

You never cry, she chided herself when she awoke on New Year's Day, 1965. A moment of clarity overcame her, and she could not immediately ignore or discard the truths that followed. *It's not that he questioned your sexuality. It was what he said about looking for something. Why? Why does that hurt so? And you're drinking far too much.*

The moment passed. The children came home. She didn't know why she went back to Frank's piano bar in the early spring. She was deliberate in her choice of seats, picking one where she could only see the sculptor, the maker of panthers, peripherally. *One drink, a couple of show tunes, and I'll go.* The waitress brought her a cognac, and she had just begun to savor the ultra brandy favor on her tongue when the young woman came back to her side and handed her a note.

It was inside a folded napkin, the script black and masculine. "I'm sorry," she read. "May I give you Resting Panther as a peace offering?"

The turn of her head was involuntary, and those eyes waited for her reply. *I know you,* they seemed to say. *It's okay.*

She didn't hesitate for a moment. She left the nonchalantly crumpled napkin in its pathetic shame on the bar, took a drop of cognac and a sweet sip of Coke in silent scorn, and left the bar with a rigidity of posture that conveyed her disdain. Twenty years would pass before she remembered why she hated any fleeting memory of the exquisite carving she had once coveted. It was not that she felt insulted; it was just that he knew. The sculptor knew she was searching for Something.

SARABANDE
WITH THE SLASHER

The sobs awakened her. Sniffles—as from one of the three young children conditioned not to leave their rooms in the middle of the night—had aroused her to a fugue state some unmeasured time ago. She was not maternal and began a return to complete oblivion then, but now could not sleep for the uncontained weeping.

Her mouth was dry. Without movement, she began the panicky research that was her every awakening. No blanket protected her from Southern California's chill March night. As if shifting in her sleep, she tested a bare toe against her makeshift bed, passed a hand across a nylon-clad flank and inhaled a deep breath.

Good. Judith was oriented—clothed and on the tapestry couch in her own living room, its dusty peach odor of spilled Jungle Gardenia unmistakable. She continued to feign sleep for the benefit of whoever was crying.

It's Sunday night, she reasoned. Panic began to abate. *I don't have to go to work until daytime. Let me see, I packed up the jewelry and then… No, wait. Oh, shit, I was at the beach with the Greek…*

Memory assaulted her. The kaleidoscope that was Sunday afternoon and evening pounded at her temples and churned in her belly. Nausea threatened, and Judith wanted a drink. *Oh, shit,* she thought again. *The no-class Greek. The no-class, no-balls Greek and I missed the Santa Monica exit off the Harbor and got lost and Albert had to stay here with the kids when he brought them home.*

Her gut cringed as she recalled her ex-husband's quiet words at the door. "You're ruining your life, Judith. I can't let you do that to these children."

The other woman hovered over her shoulder then. It listened to Judith's whispered scorn, calculated even in moments of extreme drunkenness to keep Mom and Dad's fights from the children. "You're going to take our little girl away from the brothers she adores? Sure you are, and then it will be you who ruins her life!" Albert was the only father her sons had ever known and shame rushed at her then, hipshot and disheveled in fake leopard jacket and wobbly Springolators. She was always ashamed when the Other Judith watched her, but still she screeched threats at the top of her whisper until Albert retreated through the front door, shaking his silvered head.

Judith's attention returned to the source of her awakened state. Either she was still drunk—and her desire for a shot told her she was not—or that wasn't one of the kids crying. Muffled, distinctly masculine moans came from the vicinity of her toes. It's Milt, she decided. The electrician she'd married briefly last year was a crying drunk and still had a key to the back door. *I need to get that from him*, thought Judith as she raised herself to an elbow and prepared to comfort the gentle man who loved her still.

Her long lashes parted. Light from the street lamp on Norwalk Boulevard paled the heavy dark and outlined the large body kneeling at the end of the pink marble table. Dull sparkles tried to reflect from baubles along its length. *I thought I rolled it all*, was Judith's last thought before her narrowing life changed again and forever.

"Don't cry, honey. It's okay," she began. One fluid motion brought her to a seated position and sent her dominant left hand to Milt's bald skull. She patted and continued her croon until her fingertips' receptors translated the sensation of thick, curly hair.

It's not Milt, they shrieked.

Adrenaline surged, jerked her upright, opened her eyes. The stranger flowed to his feet, and the black shape of his long body loomed against the shaded light of the dining room window. In the interminable seconds before either moved, Judith's senses recorded youth and rough work clothes, hooded eyes and heavy brows above a soft rag around the bottom of his face. She heard nothing, not even his breaths. He wasn't crying anymore.

Silent choreography began. Her feet slid two steps to the left, away from the coffee table that barred her escape through the living room door. The faint night-light by the fireplace in the far kitchen area was peripheral in her expanding vision. The back door was there.

He matched her steps, countering to his right, and did not move otherwise. She heard a gulp or swallow, then a long sigh. The soft sound electrified the fine hair on her arms.

Her bare left foot tangled in the Sarouk that covered a portion of the hardwood floor, stumbled her a fraction

forward. He extended sleeved arms and pale, empty hands
across the darkness between them and, as terror claimed her
and Halloween screams began of their own accord, Judith
had a bizarre thought. *Shall we dance,* her mind giggled while
her vocal chords lamented and her aberrant partner pounded
through the dining room, kitchen, and tiny family room and
out the rear door.

The Other Judith watched. *I didn't know you could scream
like that,* it observed as Judith reacted. She walked the ten
steps to the front door without taking a breath, flicked on the
porch light, opened the doors mechanically and continued
her shrieks while the intruder raced from the driveway at
the right side of the house and disappeared onto the dark
boulevard. One heavy paratrooper's boot was her final sight
of his flight.

I've stopped screaming now, she noted as she ran to the black
telephone on the dining table, its Sheriff's and hospital phone
numbers inked there by her own hand. *Good.* The dining
room light came on at a touch, and her returning vision
registered the open front door. Other Judith faded away and
she was now alone, terrified.

Judith ran to the door, slammed and bolted it, and then
remembered the one the intruder had used. Her chilly feet
flew across wood and tile and around the breakfast bar to the
back door. It stood open to the night. She secured the knob
lock and slumped against it, her heart threatening to throb
from her throat. *Safe now, safe now,* her mind sang.

"I've had an intruder. Please come at once," she told the
Norwalk Sheriff's substation in her professional voice and
fretted at the time it took to answer their dispassionate questions. While she waited, she thought of the Greek and his

mass of curly hair. Oily hair, she remembered, and raised her left hand to her nostrils. There was a faint odor of something like the boys' Brylcreem, and a brush across her cheek evoked a shudder with its suggestion of grease. She pawed through the stack of paper at the telephone for the man's business card.

"Yeah," he answered, obviously roused from sleep in his bed four freeways away. She could still see his stocky body with the love handles and matted black chest hair all the way to his groin; the deep, scabbed fingernail scratches on his back. She thought of the Metaxa she had spilled on his Danish Modern coffee table. It probably still lay there, a sticky mess for someone to clean on Monday. Its thick, brandy bile flavor rose now in her throat, and she could not speak. She shivered with self-loathing and hung up on his hellos, then jerked as the instrument pealed against her hand.

"Hello. Hello!" The female voice tinkled in the air as Judith snaked the receiver up from the floor and sank into a red maple dining chair to answer it.

"Judith Reeves? You called about a prowler? Our car cannot find the address. Will you repeat it, please?"

So much for quick response, was her thought as the dispatcher's apology tried to convince her it was Judith's fault the house numbers were transposed. Complaining toes sent her to the bedroom for bunny slippers while she waited for the sheriff's car that was somewhere in her neighborhood. *They look funny with this red and black Kabuki outfit*, she thought, *but it's just cops coming.*

There were two of them, uniformed, polite as they stood in her living room. The younger one wrote on a clipboard while she told them what happened and answered his questions. Yes, about ten minutes ago. No, I don't wear a watch. No, he was white. No, he wasn't stealing; he was crying, kneeling right there and sobbing. Yes, it was a rag, like a tee shirt. Well, it just felt like it. No, I didn't touch his mask; I just got that impression. No, I haven't checked to see if anything is missing. The jewelry? It's costume jewelry. I do party-plan demonstrations for extra income.

The other, fortyish deputy was rooted and silent. His eyes catalogued everything in the lighted living and dining rooms. They returned often to Judith, and she became uncomfortably aware of her voluptuous body in its lounging pajamas and incongruous pink slippers. "May we look at the rest of the house now?" Disdain and disbelief rang through the elder deputy's routine words.

One of the double-hung windows over the kitchen sink was fully open. "Look," she pointed. "That's how he got in. See, stepped on the sink and over here on the breakfast bar and down." Her purse sat in its accustomed place on the bar, the red wallet partially exposed in its drawstring opening. The cops were murmuring to each other about attempted robbery and drug users.

"No, no!" She wanted them to understand about the haunted stranger with whom she'd shared the midnight dance. "Look! He stepped right over these prescription bottles." She pointed to the pills she took for allergies and premenstrual tension. "A user would have just scooped them up.

"And, see?" she went on. "He must have seen the purse in the night-light out here. Wouldn't he have taken the wallet?" She exposed the few dollars in its bill compartment as she spoke.

The young deputy didn't answer, still scratching facts on his clipboard. The other one returned from his quick tour of the two tiny children's rooms and bathroom. "Your kids sure sleep sound," he monotoned as his narrow eyes appraised her again. "All that screaming and everything?"

Their house tour complete, the deputies returned to the living room. In their wake, she excused herself to the bathroom. She hadn't seen herself since she left the house at noon yesterday for a first brunch date with the moneyed man she'd met at a Long Beach club last weekend. Her bedroom eyes were mascara-smeared, the dark, teased hair tangled from sleep and worse, but she still looked good. Older than thirty-one, though, she told herself as she dried her hands and went back to face the minions of the law.

The clipboard was still at attention, but Unbeliever was slouched in her Victorian rocker, his cap on a crossed knee. "It could be a Metro walkaway," Clipboard argued feebly, while he thumbed down through his records. Metropolitan State Hospital for the Insane was just a few miles straight down Norwalk Boulevard. "You remember, Chris? We had that call two nights ago? Just up the road? The woman who woke up to a man standing over her bed?"

"Did she say anything about crying, kid? Sobbing? Did we find any evidence of an intruder?" The seated man's sneer quieted his partner, who waited for his senior to finish the interview.

"So, what about this guy you called and found him home? Why did you call him?" The slitted eyes didn't leave Judith, now seated across the room on the sofa. His russet hair was coarse, marked from the rim of his cap, and she imagined the stab of the stubble on the near side of his neck. Shuddering, she took a deep breath and was immediately sorry, for her breasts strained against the Kabuki jacket.

"Well, it was my first date with him this afternoon, and he did have curly hair and my address." Judith was not going to tell all. "And, well, he made a violent pass at me."

The seated man erupted, then interrogated through spasms of laughter. "Violent pass! Violent pass? What exactly does that mean, violent pass?"

She tried to explain. "Sorry. Family joke, between my sister and me. It just means, you know, like unwanted attention…" She wondered if he was going to break the rocker before his roars subsided.

His partner looked nervous and asked his first direct question since their return to the living room. "Can you think of anyone else it could possibly have been?"

While she reiterated the fact that it was a sobbing stranger, he tidied up his papers and made a move to the door. His partner sat, unflinching in the fragile chair, cap on his knee and weasel's eyes on Judith.

She stood and so did he, an eerie caricature of her earlier encounter that caused her to seat herself at once. He replaced his hat with exaggerated care and gestured at Judith and about the room.

"Tell me, Mrs. Reeves," he quizzed. "Is it your habit to lounge around in revealing outfits all the time?"

"We'll turn the report in to the detectives," Clipboard interrupted from the open door, where he was now anxious to extricate himself. "You'll hear from them in a day or two." He leaned forward to hand her a card. His partner crossed the room and pretended not to hear Judith's astonished defenses—she was covered neck to ankle in Kabuki jacket and pants, every drape and blind in the house was drawn, and why did he ask that? He did not muffle his parting shot as she closed the door behind them.

"Violent pass, indeed! Now I've heard everything."

She told the children there had been a burglar, and the policemen, our friends, had everything under control. All three were noncommittal as they ate corn flakes and packed their school lunches, their silent childhood insulating them from anything as remote as a nighttime robber. The office where she was so valuable understood that she'd slept very little and would look for her at one o'clock. She pounded temporary nails into the kitchen windows, called the landlord to ask for immediate bars on them and a deadbolt on the back door, and tried to take a nap. Judith didn't drink on the weekdays and did not make an exception now, but she was glad she didn't keep it in the house. Still trembling, she bathed and dressed in a tailored skirt, blouse, hose, and heels to leave for her East Los Angeles job at noon.

Her first new car, a '65 Dodge demonstrator on which she'd made thirty-four of thirty-six careful payments, sat in the single parking area behind the house. The registration, always to be visible on the steering column according to California law, lay ominously on the front seat. Its coiled wire frame was elongated, sprung when ripped from the post. Fear assailed her once more, and she went limp against the unlocked driver's door. She had bolted the front door, she knew. Now she scurried back and tested the rear. Satisfied, Judith headed over to Washington Boulevard with the ravaged registration bobbling on the bench seat beside her.

"Yes, I'm the detective assigned to your case, Mrs. Reeves," the smoke-damaged voice on the phone answered.

"Attempted robbery, it says here. We haven't gotten to it yet, of course…" Judith could tell he was piqued that she'd called him so soon after the incident.

"No, sir," she pandered, "I'm just calling with more information," and she went on to tell him about the car registration. "He wasn't a thief, sir. He was crying, for God's sake. This is how he finds out if a single woman lives in the house." Judith was well-informed about California's community property laws. Only a single woman had a car registered in her name alone. The detective interrupted her request that they take fingerprints.

"Says here 'attempted robbery,' ma'am. And we'll be looking into it the next day or two. Was there anything else?"

She laid her head on the desk and wanted a drink. A clerk came to the glass door and rapped, concern on her homely face. Judith looked up and bequeathed a smile, waved her eloquent hands that everything was just fine and busied herself with the day's work. She took a circuitous route as she neared home that Monday evening, afraid to pass the temptation of her Friday night watering hole.

Judith slept little on Monday night. She paced the house, checked the doors and smoked many cigarettes, the new one lit from the tip of the last. She made it home by her new route on Tuesday to discover locks on the kitchen windows and a deadbolt on the back door. The crippled registration was again wired to the steering column of the locked Dodge behind her house, and her shakes were gone on Wednesday. She told the sitter to be extra careful and took her jewelry out to La Mirada for a successful party. The hostess served a champagne punch, which Judith declined.

She didn't expect to hear from detectives and so was not surprised. By Thursday, she was reasonably calm and anxious for the weekend. The memory of the sobbing intruder was now relegated to the compartments of her mind where she kept the other chaos of her life. She skipped into the house after work that day, newspaper scooped up from the front yard, and started the rice dish the kids loved.

Judith scanned the back page of the paper while the skillet simmered. Bobby Kennedy would announce tomorrow if he was going to challenge President Johnson for the Democratic nomination. She read the whole article, and then turned to the front page.

CLUES SOUGHT IN DEATH OF WOMAN HERE, she read. Body of partially clad librarian, sexually assaulted and strangled on Wednesday night, discovered Thursday at noon. The librarian lived alone, it said, and the newspaper slid from Judith's paralyzed hands.

Her midnight dance partner had stopped crying and made up his mind. She knew it, as surely as she knew she needed a drink. She shut off the burner, grabbed her purse and called to the TV-glued children from outside the back door.

"Going to the store. Back in a minute." She hurried to the car before the older boy insisted on accompanying her, drove straight to the Serene Room and started the weekend.

She called in sick early Friday morning and yelled at the kids for eating all the macaroons after their rice the previous night. When they were off to school, she phoned Martha. "I want to move out to Santa Fe Springs. Right now. I know it's mid-month, but I'll bet we can find something. I'm coming out. Make coffee. No. No drinks. Let's find me a house first." Martha was her best friend but you had to catch her early because she drank every day now.

It was an empty pink stucco tract house not more than half a mile from Martha's. They went back to Martha's kitchen to phone the number listed in the brown front yard. It was $175 per month, first and last, and fifty more than she paid for the little house she'd lived in for over four years. She could move in tomorrow if her references checked out. "I'll probably take it; call you tomorrow," she told the eager owner and gave him her work reference and driver's license number.

They got pleasantly tipsy on Martha's endless pints of Ripple. Her friend talked against the move. "He's long gone, Judith. He'll never darken your door again, especially if he's the killer. The rent's too much. You'll have to get money from Milt just to move in, and you like your little house. And the kids should stay in their school."

Judith's courage returned with each pink glassful, and she grew determined not to be driven from her home. *I don't want to have to borrow from Milt, anyway*, she thought as she stopped at the Whittier Downs liquor store for a pint of sour mash bourbon. *I'm staying home this weekend*, she excused herself. *I may want to fix a drink.*

The voice from above her shoulder reminded her: *You don't drink in front of the kids.* "Shut up," Judith breathed aloud as she turned into her driveway and consigned Other Judith to one of the last empty compartments.

Friday's paper had a follow-up story on the librarian's murder. It called the killer the Uptown Slasher and there were no clues. Slasher? Judith marveled at the license used by the media. 'Strangler' wasn't gory enough, she decided, and went to call the neighbor/sitter to say she was home early and not going out again.

The bottle went under the pillow on her single bed. She started spaghetti sauce, put a load in the washer and thought of the drink she would fix when the kids were in bed. The three trooped in the back door, wary on Friday afternoon, and their delight in seeing her squeezed at her heart. *Shut up*, she thought at the silent voice. *Just shut up.*

She played Patterns with the boys, games she'd drawn on endless pieces of typing paper and given one of them for Christmas. The little girl wanted stories, stories, and more stories and was soon asleep, grubby and smiling at her dreams. Endless minutes passed, and nine o'clock finally arrived.

"It's the Smothers Brothers, Mom. They're really, really funny. Can't we stay up until ten, please? There's no school tomorrow." She was warm with self-sacrifice as she acquiesced, reheated the coffee and picked up the book she'd been reading for weeks. Soon she was drawn into the television program by the boys' rollicking laughter.

These Smothers Brothers are hilarious, she observed. *Funny. I never heard of them.* Somewhere between the skits about cougars in crevasses and who Mama liked best, Judith made a decision. *I'm not going to drink anymore. I'm not going to drink even on the weekends. I used to read two or three books a week, for Chrissake, and never took a sick day. I wouldn't have to sell jewelry if it wasn't for my bar tab. I could spend more time with these good kids who didn't ask to be brought into the world. And I could probably meet a nice, normal man.*

Her sons hugged her goodnight at ten o'clock and firmed up Judith's resolve. *I'll give the jug to George and Martha,* she told herself as she went to the Dodge and put the unopened bottle into its trunk. *The kids and I will stay here and face the world. Now I'm going to finish this book.* She read for an hour, moving from the sofa once to refill her coffee cup and put the last load in the dryer.

The knock didn't even startle her, although it had been months since Milt paid a late-night visit. It was a staccato shave-and-a-haircut on the locked aluminum screen door. She laid the paperback face down on the brown cushion, turned on the outside light and opened the solid wood door.

His clothes were different, a plaid shirt with white tee shirt showing at the throat, but she would know the eyes anywhere. A brown sack rustled and gurgled under his windbreaker and the ruddy neck was shaved and raw. Judith was speechless as he stood in the overgrown yard and smirked.

"I know it's late but saw your light. I thought maybe I'd come by and try to make a violent pass at you," the deputy announced. He began to ascend the steps, self-confidence in every move.

"Go away," she breathed as she slammed and bolted the door. "Go away or I'll call—I'll call—" She slid down the wall and slammed her hands against her ears.

Sometime after midnight, Judith Reeves went to the storage shed for the moving boxes and began to pack. On her second trip to the shed, she detoured to the trunk of the Dodge. Other Judith did not speak then, or again.

MR. AMES
AND THE TERRIBLE,
AWFUL, DISGUSTING
AZTEC NECKLACE

THE SIXTIES WERE DRAWING FINAL BREATHS AT M.I.T. AND in L.A. County and on the corners of Haight and Ashbury, but they'd barely arrived in Spokane County, Opportunity Township, State of Washington. "And that's not all bad," I mused. "They're iffy about hiring or renting to divorcees, but the air is clean and the rents are reasonable.

"And," I continued in the counting-my-blessings vein with which I tried to brighten this first day of spring, 1970. "Even though women can't sit at the bar, and you can't buy beer in the grocery store on Sunday, the schools have real curricula and no drug dealers!"

Everything's relative, right? Well…no. The fool who was about to call was relative to no one. No human one, at any rate.

His voice was prissy.

"Mrs. Rieck?"

"Speaking." (I answered to any of my children's surnames. It saved time.)

"This is Mr. Ames, principal of Central Valley High School."

An ominous pause ensued. Unable to outwait him, I broke the silence. "Yes?"

"Now, Mrs. Rieck, I have asked, and then told Marcus not to wear that necklace to Central Valley High School..."

I was more than polite. I pandered. My obstinate, gifted boy's high school education was too iffy to take chances. "Oh, the Aztec medallion. Sorry, Mr. Ames, does your school have a dress code against boys wearing medallions?"

Logic was the wrong approach. I could hear the froth at his mouth. "No, ma'am, we don't. I also don't have a dress code that says the boys have to wear trousers, but I'm going to expel them, anyway, if they don't!"

He continued in his little-piece-of-power-syndrome voice, but I drowned it out with the silent recitation of my new creed, the Serenity Prayer. What did it say about—oh, yes, accept the things I cannot change. And have courage to change the things I can.

Emboldened, when he paused for breath, I interjected, "Mr. Ames, what about your Roman Catholic boys? Don't they wear their St. Christopher medals?"

That tore it. Saliva flew through the phone. It was obvious to Mr. Ames that I was as ignorant of the rules of common decency as was my smart-mouthed progeny. And, since Marcus was not a practicing Aztec, he would not wear the necklace again or Mr. Ames would sever my son's relationship with Central Valley High School. Permanently.

"It's not fair, Mom!" moaned the kid that night, mouthing the battle cry of most teenagers and all emotionally retarded adults everywhere. "Everyone wears them in Los Angeles. They're just twenty years behind the times here."

I silently repeated the Serenity Prayer and reasoned with his angry heart and deaf ears. "Marcus, you're just like me.

You challenge authority when all you have is a shaky leg to stand on, just to be doing it. I've learned lately to pick my battles, save my energies for the good fight and, most of all, for the good fight that I can win." I stood tall to ruffle his wiry, blond hair. "We can't win this one, son. He's the Big Kahuna, and you are flat expelled if you don't comply."

I never saw the Aztec medallion again. Maybe it went with the boy down the road, when he quit school and began his long, tough journey in the world. Perhaps it now languishes, tarnished, in the man's keepsake box. It should be wrapped in the front-page feature story in the Spokane daily's last issue of 1979.

The article was entitled "Spokane County's Ten Stupidest Public Figures of the Decade." Our old adversary figured prominently. It seems Mr. Ames expelled the wrong kid for not cutting his terrible, awful, disgusting shoulder-length hair in 1971. A subsequent lawsuit reinstated the student and exposed the soon-to-be ex-principal for the pedantic bully he was.

I learned a lot in the years of that decade. Still, I replayed the Aztec Medallion event over and over again in my mind, coming off the humble heroine each time and fantasizing my firstborn proudly accepting his diploma with the spotlight glistening on the faux gold at his neck. I can only wonder how the man might now remember it. Dear God, I hope he knows that I did not then have the wisdom to know the difference.

THE $25 MIRACLE

SPOKANE, WASHINGTON, DECEMBER, 1969. OUTDOORS, COLD
and brown. Indoors, cold and frightened in the privacy of
my own room, away from the teenagers. Six months sober,
I'd been fired for the first time in my life at Thanksgiving. I
had to draw on California's unemployment, which was great
because I'd get $53 per week and the Washington max was
$42. Not so great, because the checks kept not coming. Not
coming, and Christmas was.

The week before Christmas, I took out everything
I'd bought and squirreled away in the linen closet during
the year. The pitiful hoard consisted mostly of socks and
short shorts, picked up at after-season sales. I enlisted the
daughter's aid in wrapping for her two older brothers. Single
socks tubed up in funny papers soon brightened the hearth.
I wrapped her pair of panty hose in Li'l Abner, and a pair of
pale green shorts in Andy Capp.

The kids always bragged that we ate best when we were
poor: biscuits and homemade hotcakes and the "rivels" that

added substance to potato and onion soup. Our kitchen boasted milk and flour, potatoes and onions, and three or four remaining strips of bacon for flavor. My purse contained four dollars.

It snowed Thursday night—lots and lots of snow. Fourteen-year-old Douglas, mittened and muffled, went out Friday with his snow shovel. By the end of the day, he'd earned five proud dollars. Saturday morning, he pulled the old sled nine blocks down to the Christmas tree lot. He was agonizing over his decision in the five-dollar area the man had pointed out to him, when I found the cash in the mailbox.

The mailman hadn't come yet. Two tens and a five, in a battered, plain white envelope, lay in the cold metal box. I looked up and down the street. I didn't know any of these people. A few recovering folks were my only acquaintances. My mentor didn't drive, and it must have been delivered last night, for the snow was pristine at the bottom of the mailbox. I could not guess then, or now, who or what blessed us so.

Visions of a little turkey with stuffing danced in my head as the middle kid hauled the Christmas tree into the yard, three hours after leaving. "I just couldn't decide, Mom. It was important it be just right. I finally picked this one, put it on the sled and went to the man with my five dollars. Oh, Mom, the man said 'Son, I hope your family appreciates you and that Christmas tree. You take it; it's a gift from me.' Mom, I still had the money! So I went and bought Dorcas a guitar strap and Marcus a book and—well, I'm not telling anything else!" He scuttled away with his paper parcel as I took in the tree.

On Saturday night, we four decorated the grandest tree ever. The kids shopped together with five dollars each on

Sunday, while I spent the remaining ten at Albertson's. Three checks arrived from California on Christmas Eve, to very little fanfare. We were already rich.

As I search this year for the perfect recipient, just the right single mom who works and struggles and keeps on keepin' on, I wonder why I don't put more than two tens and a five in this 38th anonymous envelope. After all, the dollar has devalued several times since then, and my income at retirement was ten times that of the first miracle, in 1969. I've decided against change, however, and am sure that I am only sentimental, not cheap.

BENDEMEER'S STREAM

THIS IS NOT A FISH STORY. IT IS NEITHER A WALDEN POND philosophical essay nor an ecological exposé of yet another polluted body of water. This story is about a series of lovely coincidences that happened to a little family. Perhaps it's the story of a miracle. Why don't you decide?

I was the mother, recovered from alcoholism just a couple of years, growing up alongside my three teenagers. "To paraphrase Longfellow," I would say with a laugh, "I produced grave Marcus, smiling Douglas, and Dorcas with golden hair." Astrologically, we were all Leos except Douglas. He was the precise Virgo exception.

I wondered why they weren't all Aquarians, since water seemed to rule each of their lives. Marcus was seventeen, in hot water somewhere every day. Douglas, at the other end of the spectrum, was up to his ears in holy water, with a "call" to preach since he was twelve. At fifteen, he honored his mother religiously and considered her disintegrating atheism the personal cross he bore.

Dorcas Leigh got the dishwater. She of the golden hair and cornflower eyes grew quietly amid her noisy male siblings and irreverent, flamboyant mother. She grew. She grew and *grew*, until at thirteen she was taller and heavier than even my voluptuous self and was sick unto death of the phrase *baby fat*. "Baby sequoias, maybe," she once said, as she looked at her legs in the skirt the dress code decreed she wear to school. They were…well…unfortunate legs.

Those legs, on the 5'8" barely-teenager, were about six feet long. They began at her size nine shoes and went straight on up, with barely an indentation from the ankle to the thigh. Sturdy, they were, but sturdy is not the dream of any thirteen-year-old girl. This girl would interrupt a lively algebra discussion at the dinner table with plaintive remarks like "Oh, Mom. Why couldn't I have gotten your breasts instead of your nose?"

At home, we always sang. Our whole-family Christmas favorite was "The Twelve Days of Christmas." Douglas had a good tenor voice, down from the brilliant boy soprano he'd been, and Dorcas Leigh carried an adequate tune. Marcus intoned his line—"three-ee tur-tle doves"—with baritone, off-key enthusiasm. Either Douglas or I played the piano, and we harmonized to all the old hymns I'd learned when I was a kid, and which the two younger siblings were now singing in church. Dorcas got a guitar that Christmas, and soon was chording away and singing with her brother at the piano. She needed approval, and I got out of myself enough to tell her often how beautiful and wonderful it was to hear her pick and sing, though she was nowhere near the vocalist that Douglas was, unless enthusiasm counted double.

She came home babbling, early in her freshman year, with sheet music the choir teacher had given her. "Mom, he asked me to sing a solo at the contest, and I didn't say yes until the last minute, so there weren't very many songs left, and here is mine: 'Bendemeer's Stream.'" She was tentative, beginning to suffer from buyer's remorse. I was no help.

"There weren't any songs better than this one? Dorcas, I sang this song twenty years ago. It was *old* in 1950. Plus, it's hard to sing. I only got a 'two' on it, and the accompaniment has to be just perfect or you lose the melody. Well, we'd better start practicing, if the contest's in three weeks."

We practiced. She sang bravely each night when I got home from work. In the second week, she reminded me that the contest was on Saturday, and the bus left from North Pines Junior High at 5:00 AM. On my sleeping-in morning!

Days ran away from us. Much of the time, she sounded fine on the hairy old ballad, and I acquired some hope that she might score well enough not to dash her spirits completely. I began to prepare her, anyway, with my "first time out is for experience" speech. The text could be altered to fit almost any situation, although I still hesitated to use it for sex education.

On Friday night, in between paydays, we were in the kitchen putting dinner on the table. "Now, Mom, you haven't forgotten?" she reminded me. "I have to be at the bus at five o'clock."

"Oh, dear, is that tomorrow? I thought it was next week. I wanted to get you a new dress."

"That would have been nice," she replied quietly.

How fortunate I was to hear the longing in her voice, so that I turned in time to see the lost hope in her budget-conscious eyes. I made a spot decision. "Okay, dear girl, let's see what's in the checkbook. Fourteen dollars. I have three bucks in cash, plenty of gas, and we could get by with just milk and bread until payday. Let's go out and see what we can do with fourteen bucks."

At the mall, we found we could do a great long dress with a tieback! The exact dancing blue of her eyes topped a flowing, flowered skirt. Her legs disappeared in the changing room, and it was on sale for $9.99. Adding a new pair of nylons for a buck, we whooped all the way home to clean up her old white sandals. Happiness was two females with a new dress!

She shook me awake at 4:30 AM. "Mom, get up now. I just have to put on my dress and brush my hair, and I made some coffee for you."

I sleepwalked to the kitchen in jeans with robe on top and poured a cup of coffee. Somehow, I found myself sitting and sipping on the piano bench, facing the bedroom hallway. A single bulb lit the hall sparingly as a golden girl came toward me, accessorized by shining hair and sparkling eyes. Shadows cast the planes of her elegant bones and granted a preview of the beautiful woman she was to become.

I stood up, staggered at the revelation. She giggled and made a joke about my not knowing whether I was "gettin' up or gettin' in," and I drove her the mile to the bus in silent awe. Kissed her good-bye, wished her luck, and said the first prayer of my life.

"C'mon, God. Please let her sing as beautifully as she looks."

Saturday passed. I stuck around the house, wanting to be there when they brought Dorcas home. She fairly flew in the front door, slammed her music and some other papers down on the orange couch, and screeched, "I got a TOP ONE, Mom! I was invited to sing at the evening concert, but no one else from Spokane was staying, so I couldn't get home. Look here, what one of the judges wrote on my score sheet!" There was the judge's comment in bold, black felt pen: *What is this marvelous voice doing hiding in contralto?*

She gushed on. "Oh, Mom, I was so scared. But just as the introduction finished, and I opened my mouth to sing, I got so calm, and *I knew it was going to be perfect*." She hugged me and strutted down the daylit hallway to file her treasures away.

I suppose the golden girl was always a good vocalist. It could be said my self-involvement overlooked that fact. It's probably true that the choir teacher suspected Dorcas Leigh's potential. Logic led my life and leads it now, as I recount those probable actualities.

But, oh, I remember the five o'clock dark and the shiny girl dashing to the bus. I remember my very first prayer, and I believe. I believe.

THE FEAST

I WAS TWO YEARS YOUNGER THAN THE REST OF THE SEVENTH grade class, and determined not to do it. "I'm too young," I argued. "You have to be twelve."

Two houses of worship graced our tiny prairie town. All church-going Protestants went to the Methodist, and it was time to take instructions. My stepfather was unyielding. "You will go," he said. "They have made a special dispensation for you."

I went with giggling classmates anxious to take the next step toward adulthood: "Joining The Church." While the minister's wife droned on, I whispered to Eleanor, the girl who was kindest to me, "Do you believe in God?"

Her look of horror silenced my unbelief for years. "You'll go to hell, Judy Roberts." She moved as far away from me on the bench as possible, and shunned me for the rest of our school years.

Foxgloves were two inches above the cool ground on Saturday before the church induction ceremony. I denuded them, sneaked the leaves up to my room, and chewed their sticky bitterness under the covers after bedtime. By dawn, I was so sick I was afraid my little mother would call the doctor. Instead, she kept me in bed, and I missed the service. No one ever again insisted that I "Join The Church."

I spent six months with my biological father when I was fourteen. An uncle visited us, a Jesuit priest. Father Jerry was a regular guy, collar and all, so I accosted him on a Maryland hillside with my concerns. He gave me the dispensation for which I longed.

"Don't worry about what others think," he intoned matter-of-factly. "Live your life well. God knows if you're invited to the Feast, and it's no one else's business."

I had all my babies sprinkled, hedging my bet just in case I was wrong about the whole thing. Those baptisms were in places as disparate as San Diego and Waterloo, dispensed by strangers we did not see again, and as a knock-on-wood against the recriminations of a maybe God who could mete out searing punishments upon my generation. The babies grew tall and healthy and too soon mature, for they nurtured me as I began my decline into alcoholism. A born-again babysitter introduced them to Sunday School during my last drunken days. Soon my two youngest children were Christians.

I made a commitment to a self-help program for alcoholics when I was thirty-two. I had taken a flyer with them some years before in yet another city. There I shouted my atheism and hopelessness while they spoke of God as if It rode on each of their shoulders. This time I tuned out the Godspeak and cleaned up my life. I didn't say the prayers, and I left the meeting room if someone began to sound too religious, but I didn't drink.

My family life improved over the next three years. The children went to the same schools for more than a year at a time. I went to the same job daily, to meetings, to visit the alcoholic women in jail, and to volunteer on the telephone hotline. The children were soon teenagers, and the Christian boy was sixteen.

"I'm going to be baptized, Mom," he honored his mother. "I hope you'll come."

I was belligerent and inflexible. "No, you will not. You *are* baptized. I don't care if you have to get dunked to be a voting member of your church. You will not be baptized again."

I had spoken.

He stood at the back door in his church clothes on a summer Sunday evening. "I'm going to be baptized tonight, Mom. Please come." He shushed my raving and forbidding of the ceremony with a quiet pronouncement: "Mom, there are some things you're not the boss of."

He slipped out the door. I watched with a strange pride as he walked west. Sunbeams made a halo of his soft hair. *If there is a Feast*, I thought around the lump in my throat, *that boy surely has an invitation.*

I edited a newsletter for the sober folks and took shaky women to those rooms where hope began again to live in their lives. No longer did I stalk out when other people prayed. Life lessons came to me in strange places and new open-mindedness caused humility to become an almost-familiar word. My children excelled and prospered and sang happiness around our home.

I was three and then four years sober and had a message for other atheists and agnostics who came for help with their alcoholism. "You don't have to believe in a G–o–d who created the universe in order to reap the fullness of life," I told them, and believed every word. I thought often of Uncle Jerry's analogy of invitation to the Feast, but never repeated it. It sounded too religious.

One winter day, I ran into my mother's house and straight to the bathroom. I was paging through a Reader's Digest when I came upon a life lesson. It was at the bottom of a page, where jokes are usually printed.

Two world-renowned gourmets, one a cleric and the other an atheist, met for a meal. The food was superb, the service sublime, and each course more delightful than the last. At the end of the three-hour meal, they were replete and, leaning back, contemplated the culinary perfection. Then the man of the cloth asked his unbeliever friend this simple question:

"Now, having partaken of all this wonder, can you deny there's a chef in the kitchen?"

I sat there, jeans down around my knees. Some of the first tears of my adult life spilled onto the magazine. Visions of the wonders I had already been served in sobriety danced in my head. I was invited to the Feast!

"My God!" I am sure my first vocal acknowledgement was a prayer. "My God, I believe."

REVIVAL

I HAD BEEN ON THE PRAYER LIST OF THEIR SMALL CHURCH SO long I'd risen to the top and been in stasis for years. Now my teenagers were celebrating my quiet conversion and regular church attendance. "It's the indwelling of the Holy Spirit," the oldest member explained when I questioned my soaking wet thrill as she attended me at the baptismal service. I believed, and believed in my new life.

I tried to ignore how the church ladies didn't warm to me, didn't share music with me in choir practice or include me in conversations after services. They'd been much kinder, I thought, when they were praying for me every Wednesday! Surely, they'd soon learn my conversion from atheism was real, my much-married and scarlet past washed away with the Blood, with repentance and profession of faith.

It was my first Holy Communion. I went into the women's alcove for foot washing. The two ladies on the near side moved across the room, away from me. The facilitator was starting to read from scripture, and still I had no partner. At last, the oldest woman, already diagnosed with the Alzheimer's that would claim her, left her family and brought her angelic smile across the room to me. The small Passover meal, examining my heart before the Body and Blood—all served to fill me with God's love anew. Those other folks would come around eventually, I was certain.

But the shunning continued. I examined scripture; couldn't I be a good Christian at home? It told me over and over again that I should gather with the believers, so I did, though increasingly troubled on Sunday and Wednesday evenings. My new faith was tottering. Did I even belong here with those who'd been Christians in the womb?

Revival came, a time of rebirth for the church, Pastor said. The revival's music minister led the service on Wednesday evening.

"Every hymn is a prayer!" He infected me from the podium with his joy. "Are you feeling too sick at heart or rebellious to pray?" He picked up the magenta hymnal and waved it in the air. "I hope you bought yours at the Evangel Bookstore and didn't steal it from the church," he chuckled. "Read any hymn! Read it into your heart. God will know you are attempting to pray." We sang a lot and had a rousing good time at the service, and again in the car on the way home.

After my children went to bed, I tentatively approached the piano. I'd buy a hymnal at the bookstore, I vowed, and return this one to the church. I held it out like an offering for a moment. *I'll open it at random and read the right-hand hymn,* I told myself. Long, deep breath, and then…open.

Page 256 was a song I'd never seen before. "I am so happy in Christ today," it began. The chorus, to be sung resoundingly after all four verses, brought gooseflesh to my arms and stung my eyes with grateful tears.

"Thank you, God," I breathed aloud as I read the words. "I won't doubt again. I'll stick and stay in the certain knowledge of Your love and blessing."

I read it again:

Jesus included me. Yes, He included me.
When the Lord said whosoever, *He included me.*

SAY UNCLE, LOVE

I HAD NOT SEEN LOVE. RELATIONSHIP WAS IN A MATH LESSON, the soul kiss an allusion in the novels I devoured. I knew the asterisks that followed those black and white kisses represented something, some rapture that made me wriggle with longing to x-ray through the page. I was ten, eleven, twelve, and had no model for love.

We moved, my dispassionate parents and young siblings and I, to the neck of the woods where maternal relatives farmed. A pair of aunts existed there in quiet harness with the brothers they had wed during the Great Depression. Prairie women, they baked and birthed, drove horses and tractors, played cards on Saturday night. Rare hugs were bestowed on small children, and adults kept polite, wary distances.

Mama's little sister married young. He was an older fellow, they said, with nothing of his own. Uncle Marvin and Aunt Helen farmed his folks' home place and were poor. My father gossiped when they left our house. He said the same thing each time. When he spoke, you could hear that he'd tasted the words often.

"Now, they're a strange couple, ain't they? Marvin, he's so slow, you'd think he was a quarter of a bubble off until you get to know him. And her! No help to him, that's for sure."

Uncle Marvin moved and spoke as if each word or movement had to be a perfect thing. If he was being humorous, his deep eyes filled with raucous laughter before the fourth word left his larynx. Others scraped their chairs, went for coffee refills, grew nervous at his precise presentations. Aunt Helen waited to laugh. When he went to the kitchen or the bathroom, he patted her shoulder, cupped her cheek. Her restless eyes watched, softened at his return to a room.

It was sultry in July. I spent two weeks in the cavernous farmhouse visiting them. In the early mornings, Auntie and I and the two little kids would play hide and seek or cowboys and indians around the old buildings and the brush in the farmyard. Then we'd lie on the floor in the dining room and try to stay cool. Blackened with age and dust, her mother-in-law's massive oak furniture encircled us while we listened to stories of Grandpa Hans Peter and his sod shanty childhood.

Uncle Marvin interrupted us one day, wanting his dinner. "Honey," he drawled. "Honey. It's. Noon."

"Oh, Marv. It's so hot."

She lay. He went to the kitchen sink and washed up.

"Honey, c'mon. The. Shocks. Won't. Wait."

"Oh, Marvin. I'm so hot. Just a minute, please."

She lay. He stood a long moment, went back to the kitchen. Water pumped, sloshed.

The big pail of water engulfed her, spattering me and the little ones, who giggled and wiggled on the plank floor. She leaped up, spluttering, and flailed at him. He held her wet body at arm's length.

"Are. You. Cool. Enough. To. Get. My. Dinner. Now, honey?" He led her toward the kitchen. I saw them hugging before he headed back to the oats field. She was still dripping water on the worn linoleum.

We were coming back from the dance in town that Saturday night, the night that I saw love. They danced at the old opera house in the village that was city to such as I. I had run after my two cousins, had a pop, and listened to the discordant music. Now I dozed while the children slept around me in the back seat of the old Chevy. The enormous harvest moon sat atop the barn, and I was awake when we pulled into the farmyard.

They melded. I was about to sit up when they moved into each other's arms. Silhouetted against the moonlight battering the windshield, he kissed her forever. My eyes stung from the seeing of it. I closed them in pretense of sleep and to record the memory.

He died, too soon after their children were grown, in the West Coast city where they continued their life when farming failed. I hadn't seen them in eons, but my heart agonized when I heard the news. I had sought a carbon of their love for twenty years. I wept for her loss, and for mine.

"Your Aunt Helen is coming to visit you on her wedding trip," my mother informed me. It seemed like day before yesterday that Auntie was a new widow. How could she? I was angry and disillusioned as I fought to discard my foolish childhood image of true love. How could she? I prepared a meager meal and met the newlyweds in my driveway.

Joyous as ever, Auntie leaped from the late-model car, hugged and kissed me. "I want you to meet your Uncle Suds," she trilled. "Here, honey." She took the arm of a lanky, curly-haired man who ambled from the driver's side. "This is the niece I've been telling you about."

He moved and spoke as if each word and motion had to be a perfect thing. You'd have thought he was a quarter of a bubble off if it weren't for the laughing intelligence in his eyes.

"I'm. So. Glad. To. Finally. Meet. You," he said, while my eyes filled and spilled, and my two hands grasped both of theirs, and love was in the world again.

SELF-DEFENSE

There's nothing like hindsight, I grumbled to the summer air while I looked for a parking place on the scenic Gonzaga campus. Taking my considerable business acumen into a helping profession wasn't such a good idea, if the requirements were going to mess with my mind. The MBA-Equiv test was no problem, but this ongoing education was going to make me as batty as the touchy-feely right-brainers who were most of the staff of my current employer, the largest alcoholism treatment center under one roof in the world. I had better things to do with sunny Saturday mornings.

"Schedule me for piece-of-cake stuff, Michelle," I begged the Director of Training when I met with her. "And no stress management or anger management; I've had all that."

I had not only experienced, I had survived all that, and more. A dozen years of abstinence, introspection, and prayer had finally dissipated the rage at the core of my alcoholic persona. No longer was I an accident waiting to happen; the search for serenity dominated my days. And even this kind of negative thinking isn't good for you, I reminded myself as I looked for the basement entrance to Building G.

On that naïve day just a year ago, Michelle allowed as how she would plot an easy schedule for the new Administrative Director, and I escaped when it looked as if she were going to come across the desk and hug me. One man's Mede is another man's Persian, I always say. I had no clue as to Michelle's definition of "easy."

Through the door and facing two dozen strange, pants-suited and name-tagged women on folding chairs that surrounded a dozen mattresses, I consoled myself. Nothing could be as bad as the education conclave at the end of my first six months on the job. That one was a Saturday and half of Sunday away from home, and the course was entitled "Touching Your Inner Self," or some such psychobabble. True, Michelle was probably innocent. Who in their right mind wouldn't want a weekend at a beachfront hotel? I came away from it shaken in my conviction that I had chosen the right course for the last years of my career. There were lectures given during a background of rhythmic mood music, meditations to yet more strange music, "sharing" sessions, and near-experiments with out-of-body experience. More than my convictions took a beating. I roiled in unrest for days after my return home.

"When you leave here at noon, you will have the tools to successfully defend yourself against both frontal and rear assaults upon your person." The thirty-something instructor explained the goals of a 3.5-hour course in self-defense for the woman, and her every phrase told me she felt that man, himself, was the enemy. A young assistant, whose long brown locks contrasted sharply with the instructor's butch hairdo, stood by and illustrated the short lecture with gestures.

More sharing. Around the room, the day's students offered information about themselves: their work, their families, why they were here. Many of them mentioned a growing fear of the South Hill Rapist.

"I'm here because the training director sent me," I concluded my portion of that session. "I live in the Valley," I joked, "so I don't think I'm a target for the South Hill guy."

When all had spoken their pieces, we did some limbering-up pratfalls, indoors on the mattresses. Then Ms. Butch and her troupe of one took us to the rolling green lawn and showed us how to repel a frontal assault.

It began with screaming. What a cosmic joke. I was going to learn how to yell at the top of my lungs after spending years learning to obliterate the practice from my repertoire. We actually rehearsed. "Nooooo!" rang across the campus, the students really getting into it after a couple of tentative starts.

Straight-arming was next. "Stiffen your fingers like this," they showed us. "Make your arm a javelin and drive its point right into his eyes." Now we yelled *and* practiced jabbing our javelins into the air in front of us. Always competitive, I began to worry. Were we going to make individual demonstrations? I didn't think I could do this.

"You can't hurt either one of us," Ms. Butch guaranteed as she formed us into two lines for, yes, individual practice. "Step forward with authority, screaming as you go. If he does not retreat, give him the javelin right in his eyes. Do not falter, and don't worry. We're ready, and we always duck."

"Nooooo!" My line in front of the assistant inched forward on the soft grass whose new-mown smell permeated the air. Some praises came from both instructors—"Good yell!" and "Nice javelin!"—with a rare "Let's try that one more time." Then there were no other students in front of me.

I stood there mute, my javelin al dente. Her young eyes sought my nametag. "Come on, Judith. This guy is going to rob, rape, and murder you. Get him!"

There was only truth in my response—no flamboyance, no daring to be different, no flaunting of authority, or any of the other character defects I had worked on for such a long time. "I can't," I admitted. "I just can't do this to another human being. I guess he's just going to have to rob, rape, and murder me if I can't talk him out of it."

The line beside us stopped and stared. Their instructor left them and came over to stand at my side. "Didn't you say you had a little granddaughter, Judith? What was her name again?"

"Meagan," I answered. "Her name is Meagan. She's five."

Even today, a quarter century later, the fine hair on my dominant left arm stands at attention as I relate this part of the story of my ongoing education. In those ensuing years, I was to learn that Ms. Butch had a husband and sons, that pathetic Freddie Coe was the dreaded South Hill Rapist, and that I was one of those right-brainers I thought I despised and whom Michelle had recognized. But on that day there would be a single lesson.

"Well, Judith," she spoke from my side with unerring sympathy for my self-esteem. "This guy is now going to rob, rape, and murder Meagan."

"Noooooo!" Adrenaline surged, raised and stiffened each single hair on my neck and limbs. A red, primal force formed the javelin that tried to blind the young instructor in front of me as the scream reverberated in my ears. "Noooo!"

There is, after all, a place in the world for rage.

CREDIT WHERE
CREDIT IS DUE

"MRS. HOLUB?" A MASCULINE VOICE ASKED ON THE TELEPHONE one sweet, late May day.

"Speaking," I said, answering, as usual, to any of the children's last names.

"This is Tony Rasmussen over at CV High. I'm counselor to the Class of '74. Dorcas is here to get an early checkout slip, and the parent is supposed to sign it first. But since it's Dorcas, I thought I'd just call and make sure you knew she was going to California tomorrow morning. In a car?" He chuckled at his little joke and continued, "Here, she wants to talk with you."

"Mom! I can check out of all my classes today except typing. I have to go in and have Mrs. Smith sign me out first thing in the morning. So will you call the Keene's and tell them to pick me up at 8:30, not 7:30 in the morning?"

I assured her I'd get it handled and left the message on Maggie Keene's CodaPhone as I mused about Mrs. Smith. Seemed to be a pretty stick-up-the-butt lady, at least when I had spoken to her on the telephone three or four years ago. Back then, Marcus had agreed to take the typing class to see if he couldn't manage to get some written work done on the typewriter at home. He wasn't dyslexic and was frighteningly intelligent, but he very nearly could not write by hand. It frustrated him, and we thought perhaps typing would be his salvation.

My eldest was to discover many salvations, but alas, typing was not one of them. A few frustrating days at the typewriter in Mrs. Smith's class, and he pulled himself up to his full six feet two. With his windmill eyes whirling, he dashed the typewriter to the floor and himself to freedom. My subsequent conversations with Mrs. Smith had been limited to discussions of liability for the infernal machine.

We got busy, the sixteen-year-old girl child and I, packing and missing each other already. She was saving money by getting this hop to California to spend her annual two months with her dad. I didn't think of Mrs. Smith again until Dorcas ran up the street to the high school and back again, to check out of her final class the next morning.

"Everything okay?" I asked, placing suitcases and the baby pop cooler in front of the door, never to be forgotten.

She nodded. "Yup. And, oh, my typing teacher wants to meet you some day."

"Yeah? Why is that, honey?" I was just trading words with my golden girl, asking time to stand still, to keep her here a little longer.

"Well, she thinks you must be a very good parent, and she'd like to meet you."

Aha! Vindication for these years of trying to grow up before the teenagers. She had my attention. In my humblest manner, I casually asked, "Oh, yeah? Exactly what did she say?"

"Well, she said, 'You know, Dorcas, I had your brother, Douglas, in this class two years ago, and he was the finest student I'd ever had. Now I have you this year, and you are the finest student I've ever had. You must have wonderful parents.' When I said I only had a mom, she said that made you a doubly fine parent."

My ego demanded more. Still casual, I asked, "Then what did you say, sweetheart?"

Her reply was quiet and innocent. "I said, 'Mrs. Smith, do you remember my brother, Marcus Rieck?'"

THE CHRISTMAS CAT

THE LITTLE ANTIQUE HOUSE IN THE SUGARHOUSE DISTRICT of Salt Lake City was my birthday present to me in the summer of 1988. Every waking moment of the next four months that I wasn't at work, I fixed up the house. It was not ordinary, just-moving-in work. My first task, for instance, was to sterilize a bedroom and install a mini-refrigerator and microwave therein—a bacteria-free living space from which to expand the sterilization process outward. The previous tenants, a motorcycle bunch, must have done bike repair and major surgery in the kitchen and housed lions and tigers and bears in the living room before they boarded up the blackened fireplace, burned down the garage, and disappeared in the middle of the night.

I was grateful for the scut work. Dissolving the grease globs that hung from the kitchen ceiling, renewing the golden oak floors, toothbrushing the little ceramic tiles in the bathroom and kitchen, and revitalizing the woodwork fashioned of Utah's curl-leaf mountain-mahogany kept my out-of-office hours occupied. I had no time left for introspection, not a moment to take a breath and admit how incomprehensibly lonely I was after the divorce.

By Thanksgiving week, the house sparkled as the chimney sweep doffed his top hat and wished me happy holidays. I had left the fireplace for last, for I was truly afraid of what would be forthcoming with the boards removed. There were no bodies, though, only piles of debris. Degreaser, Spic 'n' Span, a stiff brush, and a toothbrush revealed an unrivaled marvel of a pastel-tiled, Sugarhouse fireplace. It was the *pièce de résistance.*

The sweep skipped out the gleaming front door. I sat in my Victorian rocker and wept. The house was magnificent, but what would I do now?

"Maybe I'll get a cat," was a passing thought as I got in the car and went over to one of the sober clubs I frequented. "But what if I don't like living with a cat? Can you take them back?"

The notice screaming from the club bulletin board was my answer. "Keep my house cat while I do a month in the Reserves? She's a darling." Here was a cat I could try on for size! I called the phone number, and Samantha came to my solitary home.

Calico, not young, and assuredly not darling, she weighed at least fifteen pounds and despised me at once. "She'll be strange for a couple of days—they always are," said her mistress as she threw the cat paraphernalia into the living room and escaped.

When I looked around, Samantha, too, had disappeared. Forever. She ate and pooped, presumably while I was at work or sleeping, but days passed, and I only heard her. Skitter, skitter, clump, clump. She had squeezed into an eight-inch gap in an oak floor register in the den and taken up residence in the enormous cold air ducts of the ancient gas furnace. The second week, I brought a cat trap from work and put her food in it one night, but in the morning the trap was sprung and both Samantha and the food were gone. I decided her owner would have to lure Samantha out when she got back from the army, and the cat and I began our non-physical cohabitation—I in my miserable solitude and Samantha in her air duct.

On Christmas Eve, I shut off the TV—"It's a Wonderful Life" was not my self-pitying cup of tea—and picked up a book. A Utah snowstorm was raging, so I couldn't drive to the club, and depression threatened to overwhelm me. I tried so hard to concentrate on the novel that I didn't hear her scratch her way up the duct and into the den.

Without hesitation, Samantha wrapped a skinny, be-draggled body around my ankles and purred like a fifty-horse motor boat. "Don't be sad," she crooned. "I'm here." No Child in a whole stable full of animals had been adored any more than I was at that moment. One more time, the Something that first charted my path and now guides my life had sent me a message of hope and love—this time with a transient messenger called Samantha.

STEPHANIE'S LIGHT

SHE WAS SITTING ON HER BACKPACK OUTSIDE THE "WELCOME to Oregon" rest stop, and it was beginning to rain. Hippie-type bands and jangles were incongruous on the fortyish face that asked a silent question through the open passenger's window, there on a summer Sunday in 1989.

"I'm going almost to Portland," I answered, "staying here on I-84 all the way. But I'm late for a rendezvous and can't stop for anything."

"That's great." She spoke with the innocence of a 1960's preteener, and began to pick up her stuff from the roadside with quiet precision.

"Wait a minute!" I leaned over and yelled back at her through the open window. "I smoke a lot when I drive."

"That's great, too! I also drink beer..." she toasted a previously unseen Coors Light at me.

"Well, I don't." My controller's voice, which I had vowed to leave in Salt Lake City on this week's vacation, took over. "And I can't have an open container in the car."

She upended the can, not even taking a final sip. Opening the passenger door gently so she wouldn't frighten me (*she's afraid she'll scare me!*), she presented the emptied can as if it were a nosegay to the Princess of Wales. "I'll need to put this in your trash bag," she crooned.

She reassured me, leaning to pile her backpack in the rear seat and arrange her belongings. "I'm not really a drinker. I'm into good drugs. But some folks from the Rainbow Family gathering came by, and they didn't have room for me so they gave me hugs and that beer."

"I guess you didn't see my bright orange bumper sticker?" (*Damn! Why wouldn't my Iron Lady voice stay home this week?*) "It says 'Let's Stop Drugs.'"

"Not *drug* drugs!" she continued to reassure. "Just good marijuana, and only to meditate." She patted my worn 24-hour book on the dashboard reverently. "You must meditate, so you know what I mean."

She babbled for thirty miles. Her name was Stephanie. Her house was on her back. I was only the second woman who'd ever picked her up. She had come from Jacksonville, Florida to attend the 20,000-strong Rainbow Family gathering in a national forest outside Twin Falls, Idaho. Her birthday was next Sunday, and she always got happy a week or so before. She didn't get to be a hippy in the 60's because she was raising her family (*My God! She's as old as I am!*), but they were grown now, and she'd dedicated the rest of her life to doing exactly as she pleased.

As she consulted the tattered Rand McNally from her pack to see where she'd be when I dropped her off at Cascade Locks, the hair on my left arm stiffened and rose. My exact words, I marveled. Exactly what I promised myself when, divorced and responsibility-free, I left my home of twenty years and came to land in Salt Lake City.

And continued to do as I please, I argued with myself. My too-responsible job, sweet little antique house, and sometimes possessive sweetheart are all things that I chose to acquire, am pleased to have.

She interrupted my uncomfortable reverie, offering a cello-wrapped cinnamon candy. My childhood favorite. Its taste sharp in my nostrils and glands rebelling at the suddenness of the forgotten flavor, I nearly missed the Baker City exit.

"I have to fill up the tank now, Stephanie." (*Thank you, God. This voice I am using is the one that speaks to my sister.*) "I can't stop to eat, but if there's a place close to the gas station, you could run over and get us an ice cream cone or something."

"Great! I'm starving." She returned to the car with the change from my $20 bill carefully clutched in her left hand, eating french fries in childlike abandon with her right, a bag of burgers under her arm. "I'll get drinks—my treat!" and she loped over to the Coke machine.

The Cutlass cruised at exactly 45 along the city street, anxious to return to the breezy 65 of the highway. (*I will now talk with you, Stephanie. I want to tell you about Keith's death, about the bumper sticker. There are so many things I want to know, to understand, about the way you live and think and feel. I will now open my mouth and hear the voice that loves begin to speak to a sister.*)

"Gosh! That looks like fun!" She pointed at the Lions International tents and displays in the Baker City park we were passing on our return to I-84. "Oh, my! Fun!"

Iron Lady spoke. "I'll drop you, if you want to stay, Stephanie."

"Of course. I don't mind," and she was offloaded and had made her self-proclaimed idiot check of the car and the area around it before I knew she was really leaving me. She smiled, fluttered a butterfly wave, and disappeared into the crowd.

Her Coke lasted nearly to Cascade Locks. I savored the last sticky drops as I arrived at my rendezvous only ten minutes late. I was hugged and loved and fed cinnamon rolls and apple pie by my mother's aging sisters. We spoke of the dead and the dying, and of the gas mileage in our respective Oldsmobiles. On the return trip, I watched the Columbia Gorge scenery resolutely, not discerning the size or shape of the occasional backpacked hitchhiker.

Rested and refreshed, ready to resume my life, I am home on Saturday night. I have caressed the cool strawberryness of a Royal Beyruth pitcher as I add it to my collection on the shelf. The silver Light can, destined never to become a part of roadside litter, twinkles from that same shelf. I'll pitch it tomorrow. Tomorrow is my birthday.

Happy birthday, Stephanie.

SMOKE AND FIRE

The author says:
Some years past, a fictionalized version of this story appeared at www.storyhouse.org, a third-person catharsis in which I did not admit it was I who suffered so greatly. Here it is, in all its ugliness with its lesson learned: Feelings are not facts, perception can't always be trusted, and there is no defense against the Big Lie.

REMEMBER WHEN THE AVON LADY CAME EVERY MONTH? Her basket was full of scented samples, and she appreciated my order. These days, one appears magically during the Christmas season. She hangs a couple of catalogs on my door in the middle of the night, so she won't have to see me. If I want my soap or bath oil, I have to talk to her answering machine. She could be a man, a *nom de plume* on voice mail, for all I know.

In the Cape Cod Colonial on the South Hill, mid-70's, the Avon Lady visited in the evening, bringing tidbits of gossip from the neighborhood. "I'm not sure this is true," she'd titter as she placed yet another new product in my hands, "but where there's smoke, there's fire, you know." I wasn't acquainted with them, working all day and half the weekends as I did, but my neighbors' peccadilloes became familiar to me, the only truths imprinted in my brain as to their existence. And my mama used to say that, too. *Where there's smoke, there's fire.*

"Which house does she live in?" I encouraged that Avon Lady's penchant for carrying tales in suburbia and knew my neighbors only through her. The woman in the blue house across from me was in her seventh marriage. The two guys in the house on the corner weren't really uncle and nephew. "You know what I mean..." her face downcast with titillated innocence. The redhead across the street had undergone four abortions. I thought I knew them and remembered their sins, even when I didn't live there anymore.

Career-wise, a taste of turnaround accounting hooked me; I had a special talent for procedural cleanup and cash flow management, and many small businesses were in need of my services. Divorced for the last time, I swore there was nothing to stop me from indulging my itchy trigger foot from seeking out one- or two-year jobs anywhere in the country. I searched the "Controller wanted" classifieds in out-of-town newspapers at the library, and sent my resume to those whose wording sounded like they needed me. "Hands-on, challenge, you'll never be bored," were part of my criteria in potential employer's advertisements. It worked. My un-spoken need to be needed and to have new work scenery regularly was fulfilled. A few successful years later, I found myself in Portland, Oregon.

"Our accounting staff has been with us forever," prospective employers would say, and these folks were no exception. "We'd hate to lose them. What is your track record for maintaining existing staff?"

I was always truthful, even blunt. I interviewed in nice jeans and a blazer because that was my work outfit; hands-on accounting work in a troubled company involves much digging into dirty files, and they would know they were not getting a clotheshorse. From experience, I knew that the combination of lackadaisical management and existing accounting staff were always the problem. "I'll lose about half of them," I always replied. "Half of that half won't work for me, and the other half I will let go."

They gulped, sent me out of the room, probably reviewed the glowing references in the folder on their desk, and put me to work with my new staff of seven. As in previous jobs, most of those seven had sympathies with their discharged supervisor. Two of them seemed to be deliberately making the work more difficult and my life miserable. One was the old chief clerk, who had been there forever; the other was a bright, young accounts receivable clerk whom I desperately wanted to keep at her data processing station. I was still spending a lot of time at her desk, watching the ins and outs of the convoluted cash intake and putting a pencil to new, simpler procedures that I had to implement, when the stuff hit the fan.

I knew one person in Portland: Alice, who lived with her husband down the Columbia Gorge near my two old aunties. She worked there in the city, and we lunched a couple of times a week. We were sisters of the heart, and she was a loving balm to the turmoil I always went through in the first weeks of a new challenge.

I called the two into my office at the end of the first month. "Two weeks to get on the team," I told their stone faces. "I could personally handle what you're both doing badly right now until I find other staff," I said.

"Yes, ma'am," they replied.

The chief clerk sat in her partitioned corner and smiled enigmatically, while the young one never returned to work. Our Workman's Compensation carrier had a claim within the week.

"Mental anguish. Sexual harassment. 'She rubbed against me and grabbed my chi-chi's,'" was on the copy of the hand-written claim form Personnel received.

I went to the carrier's office and met with its attorney. They were negotiating a reasonable settlement, and my company would have nothing to say about it. "It saves money in the long run," she said, and did not meet my eyes. "We don't admit guilt, of course." She smiled and judged my short hair, tweed blazer, and the smoke in the file in front of her, and did not offer her hand.

A photocopy of the claim and the payoff was on the windshield of each car in the parking lot a week later. I still didn't know if chi-chi's were breasts or buttocks when the summons came from the State of Oregon. The old girl continued to smirk in her corner. The temporary data operator shrank from me and ran to the bathroom, weeping.

We all met in the boardroom: the president, chairman of the board, corporate attorney, and me.

"Betty complained to me some weeks ago," the president finally confessed. "She said J. R. was crowding her and making her uncomfortable." At the attorney's question, he replied, "I told her something like 'grin and bear it,' and asked her to come to me again if she felt it continued. I didn't want to bother J. R. with it."

I was aghast, but measured my response. "This is the only place I will voice this," I said and gestured to include the three of them, "but you have done me—and the company—a great disservice by not telling me of this immediately. Personal space is sacrosanct, and I could have been particularly careful when working with this woman if I had known."

Perception. I thought of leaning over the clerk's shoulder to watch her computer screen, of my implant breasts that had no feeling and probably brushed her shoulder, of hugging Alice goodbye in our parking lot full of employees returning from lunch. My manner of dress, my singlehood, all these isolated bits must have combined to give this clerk a false perception of my sexuality. I did not then think of the out-and-out falsehood—the grabbing of chi-chi's—for my thoughts went to my neighbors on the South Hill, so many years before. Who were they really, I wondered? And had they been hurt this badly, also?

The old girl went down the road as I knew she would, before the date of the State of Oregon hearing. My new employer was allowed to bring the accused (me), an officer who could sign a settlement, and one other person only. This person had to be the corporate attorney, so there would be no one to vouch for my sexuality. It's too important, the president said. The State takes sexual harassment seriously.

The accuser could present as many witnesses as time allowed, and stated her case first, including the chi-chi's. "Breasts," she clarified to the mediator. She had only one witness. The bitter old girl appeared. In response to Mr. Washington's question, she replied, "No, she never touched me. But I was always careful to keep a table between us."

"I'm heterosexual, period," I testified. "It's not feasible that I harassed this woman. Check my twenty-two years' work history. Talk to the last women I supervised, or to my ex-husband." Washington heard me out, the hearing was over, and he ushered our party into a side room.

We ventured small victory smiles. There was no proof, all we've lost is valuable time, our cautious expressions reassured one another. The attorney was making notes in her file when the mediator returned. "The plaintiff will accept a check now for $25,000 in full settlement."

"I'm guilty?" I asked.

"Without proof on either side, we choose to err on the side of the wronged," Mr. Washington intoned as from a prepared script.

Wronged? I could hear him thinking about smoke and fire as I stumbled down a strange hallway to find a bathroom and vomit.

Give my president credit. He replied on the order of "millions for defense, not a cent for tribute," the case was remanded up the Oregon ladder, and I went back to work. A shaky, not-like-me work, in which I trembled when I had to work closely with one of the women and perceived censure in the eyes of all but a few. Disbelief turned to anger at Mr. Washington, the State of Oregon, and their perception of who was wronged; my sharp mind became stuffed with scarlet cotton. I was useless at my desk, and my daily medicine of prayer and meditation did not alleviate my rage. Finally, I called our health insurance carrier.

"The insurance pays half of the visits," I told the president. "I think you guys owe me the other half. Or I'll have to leave. I'm no good to you the way I am."

He grinned, this kind, supportive man. "Well, we're not talking years of intensive psychotherapy here, are we, J. R.? I'm sure the company can pop for a few visits to a shrink."

She was actually a child and family therapist, and she let me rage and weep the whole first fifty-minute hour in her large, casually cluttered office, eliciting a few tidbits of information on my twenty years of attempted spiritual growth during times of nose blowing and taking a breath. Half the second visit was a repeat of the first. Then she stopped me, forcefully.

"Your anger is directed at the mediator and the State," she observed. "You have not once mentioned the clerk who started it all. Why, I wonder?"

I started to explain to her what we did about resentment— pray for all good things for the person, for thirty days. "On the day I saw the photocopies on the windshields, I got on my knees and began to pray for all good things for Betty," I began. And the light dawned.

"Oh!" Self-assured me returned in a flash, dripping nose and all, and I practically took over the session. "I need to pray for all good things for Mr. Washington and the State of Oregon," I said, omitting the sailor language I had been using to describe both. "I'll come back one more time, but I don't think I'm going to need any more psychotherapy."

I didn't. Nearly two years later, remarried to my soul mate and on another tough job in Washington State, the phone rang one evening. It was that kind president, reporting that I had been fully exonerated on that day, in the higher Oregon appeals process.

Do not protest too much, my well-worn morning meditation book tells me. *Do not protest, whether accusations be false or true. Only your God can judge the real you.*

It is a comfort, but I must add this: I do not encourage, will not repeat, and shall not perpetuate rumor or gossip of any nature. Each time the media clamors or an acquaintance whispers, I close my ears and remember the pain.

Smoke and fire ain't what it used to be, Mama.

Siah, R.I.P.

SHE LOVED HER CATS AND KITTENS EVEN MORE THAN SHE liked me. In retrospect, it is entirely possible that my little sister viewed me and my reading in the same light. I hid from my dysfunctional home with my nose in a book, except at table where reading was *verboten*. Sister Nancy lavished her sweet heart on dogs and horses and cats. Especially cats.

I escaped the loveless prairie household before I was sixteen, leaving her and her feline friends to fend for themselves against the stepfather monster, our silent beauty mother, and a spoiled young half-brother. Without a backward glance, I began an emancipated life, accumulating husbands, children, and homes in several states. In none of my houses were animals welcome; none of my children were allowed to have pets. Especially cats.

A dozen years passed. Sister Nancy came from Idaho with her husband and small daughter to relocate in Southern California. They stayed with us for a short time, the trailer with their possessions parked behind the house. It was three or four days before I realized my sister was making many trips out the back door, sometimes with a dish held surreptitiously in front of her. The light bulb flashed in my brain. A cat, of course.

"Nancy," I yelled, not gently. "Do you have a cat out in that trailer?"

She put on her best baby face. Her eyes twinkled. "Sister," she cooed, "would I bring a cat to your house? A mother cat with several tiny kittens? Would I do such a thing?"

She was impossible to resist when she was teasing. "Well, I don't really care," I told her. "But they can't come in the house."

Nancy and family soon had their own house, and the kittens were weaned. One Saturday, she dressed her Shirley Temple look-alike daughter in the child's best Kate Greenaway frock and sent her out in the neighborhood with a basket of kittens—three of them, cute and roly-poly. Little Katherine returned an hour later. Four cute kittens now cuddled in the basket. My sister just chuckled. "The more, the merrier," she insisted, and didn't try to give one to me.

Our paths diverged again, and another dozen years went by. Divorced and living in eastern Washington State, Nancy finally found her best friend. *Rimrock's Siah of Beth-Al* was a very spendy, smoked black Persian with a pushed-in face. And Attitude. Nancy's original idea was to make piles of money in the Very Spendy Kitten business, and to this end she took Siah to be bred as soon as the regal Persian was the proper age.

Rimrock's Siah of Beth-Al didn't care for the process. Didn't care for it at all, and at the top of her royal lungs. After a couple of extra days, the cattery gave up. Siah was not going to provide miniature push-faced dollar signs in this lifetime.

Nancy didn't mind at all, gaga as she was over the black queen. She just had Siah spayed and continued to lavish attention and affection on her.

I was maturing and mellowing, although I remained a slow learner of life's lessons. My children were teenagers, but there were still no pets in my house. I remember being awestruck at a time when Nancy was temporarily without funds and had just enough coins for a pack of cigarettes. She returned from the store with a carton of cottage cheese for Siah and a pack of gum. I voiced my disgust at the time, but can still call up the feeling of admiration that engulfed me at her selfless act. Oh, how she loved that cat.

Robert joined their twosome. His work took him around the west coast and the three of them, litter box and all, lived for weeks at a time in her square, old Volkswagen van. They dreamed of buying property and settling down somewhere, and took a sight-unseen option on some land near Bakersfield. Siah grew old and began to spend more and more time with the veterinarian.

The children grew and flourished and left home.

I acquired a cat.

It was a fluke, a comedy of unbelievable errors and omissions, but I had a cat. He was a small, brown Burmese with fur as soft as mink. His purr lulled me to sleep each night, and his rough tongue awakened me each morning. He turned up his nose at cottage cheese, but a month had not elapsed before I knew I would forego cigarettes to get it for him if he wanted it. Finally, I had a housemate who wouldn't leave me.

This was my altered state of mind when I opened Siah's death announcement that winter. Nancy's dear friend passed

away while Robert was working a job in Las Vegas. I laid
my head on the desk and cried, the little hand-written card
clutched in my fist. My poor sister. I didn't ever want to learn
how terribly she grieved.

Nancy was determined to bury Siah on her own land,
so they put the body on dry ice in a picnic cooler. It sat in
the same place as the litter pan they no longer needed in the
van, but occupied more space in those cramped quarters.
Robert's work in Las Vegas ended a few weeks after Siah's
death. Robert, Nancy, Siah's dry-iced body, and the van
headed for California.

My scalp crawled when she called to tell me of the
Bakersfield experience. "It was horrible, Seester," she said.
"It was about twilight when we got there, and the land that
was supposedly ours was moving. Moving, swaying back and
forth, like a bad dream. The road ahead moved, too. It was
huge spiders! Tarantulas, I think, and bazillions of them."
Nancy refused to step out of the van and insisted that her
husband forfeit the option monies.

Patient Robert was dedicated to my sister's happiness.
Nancy's last words in that phone conversation were, "We're
headed for Spokane. We'll bury Siah at Kitty's place." The
Shirley Temple child was now an adult Jamie Lee Curtis look-
alike with a home and child of her own. The Volkswagen
van, dry ice replenished, turned around to begin the long
trip north, to eastern Washington State. I gave CoCoa an
extra tablespoon of treat for his dinner and more petting
than usual when we retired that night.

If you are unfamiliar with Washington State, your
immediate thought when you hear it mentioned is, "It rains
all the time." Then perhaps you think of lush ferns, beaches,

and forests of cedar and pine that soften the first, wet image. This is only 50% correct. This description is of western Washington, from Puget Sound to the towering Cascade mountain range that divides the evergreen state. Eastern Washington, while not devoid of its own evergreens, is a plain of contrast. Arid desert land, then the lush farmland of the gentle Palouse hills greets your eyes when you cross the wide Columbia, its ancient power dammed to all but the imagination. A stone's throw east of Spokane is the Idaho panhandle, and the mountain passes that lead to Montana. Nestled between the two rocky heights, eastern Washington has sun and rain in equal proportions. It boasts fields of wheat in summer to boggle the mind, stone houses, stone fences, stone walls. And clearly defined seasons. Hot summers, frigid winters, sweet springs, and autumns that take your breath away.

It was February at Kitty's, frigid winter. Robert could not get a shovel into any of the frozen earth in her yard. Siah's final resting place was not going to be in Spokane, not that year.

"Robert has to go back to Vegas," my sister reported on the phone. Siah's beloved body had mummified in the ongoing weeks, and dry ice was no longer a necessity. "We'll find property somewhere," Nancy determined. She sent Robert off to the pawnshop.

They wrapped her with loving care, placed *Rimrock's Siah of Beth-Al* in the nice, nearly-new suitcase Robert brought home, and strapped it carefully to the back of the van. Discarding the cooler made the Volkswagen's interior seem roomy after living over and around it for so long. They took turns driving and, just before dawn, found themselves near Las Vegas. Robert pulled into a Denny's. Nancy patted Siah's suitcase as she passed by to go to breakfast.

The couple ate leisurely, spoke of areas where they could buy land, and of the stone Nancy would paint for Siah's grave. When they returned to the parking lot, the unbroken lines of the Volkswagen's boxy rear greeted them, startling their joint imagination.

A thief had lurked in the night. The suitcase was gone.

BOOGER

AN ENORMOUS, WILD CAT WAS THE SOLE OCCUPANT OF OUR five-acre property when we moved onto it. We'd see him streaking from the barn across the pasture at dusk. Tall and skinny, long-furred and white with a strangely flat, black tail, he would race from one hiding place to the next while he checked us out. I was worried that my tiny CoCoa, a gentle Sable Burmese, was in danger of contracting some dread disease from the Wild One.

We vacationed in San Diego a couple of weeks after moving in. While we were gone, my son-in-law was to add skirting to the mobile home, and the daughter's only job was to trap the wild cat and take it to the pound.

"There were bird carcasses under the trailer," son-in-law told us when we stopped there on the way home. "That old boy must stay under there sometimes." Daughter had to reserve a cat trap from the County, and she said they would call when one was available.

We arrived home at dusk and decided to pick CoCoa up from the cat kennel the next day. Unloading the pickup and carrying armloads of travel debris up the back path to the deck, we heard, "Meow! Meow!"

My tone-deaf husband perked up his ears. "Is that a quail?"

"No!" I screeched. "It's a cat, and it's probably that wild cat, trapped under the trailer!" But we didn't hear it again, so we put on a pot of coffee and went to the truck for another load.

"Meowrrrw!" It was louder now and came from the rear. There was the big cat, leaning up against the wire fence that separated the back yard from the outbuildings. It called to us again, most certainly complaining, "Where have you been for two weeks? Where is my little brown playmate?" As I tiptoed gingerly toward the fence, he flopped against the wire, clearly trying to give me his belly through the barrier. I scratched it with a tentative index finger.

Dale, who irreverently calls my Burmese "Brownie," got in a belly-scratch, too, and issued an invitation. "Well, come on, Old Black-and-Whitey; come for a visit."

Tail in the air and walking proud, our new friend followed us onto the deck and into the house for a gobble of dry cat food. He didn't want to be a house cat, though, no matter how excellent the cuisine. When Dale closed the door after the last bag of laundry was in the house, the big tom's white face with the large black dot under its left nostril went feral. He deserted the food dish in a flash and climbed every wall and cupboard at the top of his lungs until we opened the door again. Then he fled into the night.

By summer, our relationship had progressed. He began to fill out to the size and strength of a small bobcat and came to visit nearly every other evening. He'd devour a dish of food on the deck and beg for a few strokes. On one occasion, Dale said, "Look at his face. We should name him Booger! We can't keep calling him Old Black-and-Whitey."

"We can't name him anything, honey," I insisted. "He's not ours."

But I started putting more worm medicine and yeast tablets in his food. On the rare occasion that I'd see the little brown guy in the pasture with the Wild One, I'd just pray for CoCoa's health.

One day, the County called. A sweet voice said, "We have a trap available for you now. You know, for trapping your wild cat?"

I didn't know whose he was, where he lived, or what terrible diseases he might be carrying, but I knew I loved his freedom. I didn't hesitate. "No, thanks," I said. "We've discovered Booger's not wild, after all."

LOST AND FOUND

I GOT ON A PLANE AND WENT TO WORK IN A CAMPAIGN A thousand miles away. Packed a bag and left my indulgent husband with the details, as usual. Some friends were moving to our town from the Coast, and they would stay in our acreage home and take care of the little Sable Burmese, CoCoa. Booger, the big white tom with the black dot on his nose whom we'd inherited part-time with the property, could take care of himself. Dale would be able to join me soon.

CoCoa was given to me at six months old. *He* was six months; I was past fifty and had never had a pet. He came already named; I would have called him Demosthenes. He drooled. He was neutered, had all his shots, and didn't need any more until he was a year old, and I knew from nothing about cats. The little brown guy's bad breath and dribbling were normal cat traits to me.

After he came out from under the refrigerator, CoCoa's training began, and he was a quick study. Soon he was sitting only on green towels, staying out of my face, and looking forward to the auto ride and the new home wherever my next job took me.

His routine, one-year visit produced an ominous forecast. "I'm going to be seeing a lot of this little guy," the veterinarian said.

CoCoa suffered from Acquired Immune Deficiency Plasmatic Gingivitis. Translated, it meant two to three hundred bucks every time he got "down" with it, which was a couple of times a year. He was mine (or I was his?), however, so I made the commitment to keep his life as comfortable as possible. Yes, I loved him. I loved him with the fervor I used to deplore in my sister, The Cat Woman, and all those lonely women who baby-talk their paranoid little animals.

So I flew away, five years and fifteen hundred dollars later. My husband was to join me soon, and we would drive home together.

The doorbell rang at 5:30 AM in my temporary home, a little furnished row cottage. Anxious after three weeks of sep- aration, I threw open the door to greet my weary husband.

And CoCoa! The friends had decided not to move. Dale could find no one to stay at our place, and I couldn't keep a cat in the rental! We took him to an acquaintance who was a cat lover. Her home was sans cat right now. She had a lordly little Shitzu, Larry.

"Larry just loved Jack-Cat," she told us, and I believed it. "I'm sure there'll be no dog-cat problem."

We visited our little brown guy on the weekend. He was cool, even as he allowed himself to be brushed and stroked. My friend said he stayed under the stereo until she came home at night, and slept with her like Jack-Cat used to. I didn't know my last glimpse of him would be the disapproving look he gave me as I brushed him away with my foot when he tried to follow us out the door.

CoCoa found a way out, as had Jack-Cat before him, through the window insert around the air conditioner. He was gone when she came home on Monday to a smiling Larry, king of his domain again.

We combed the neighborhood. We walked a mile in each direction, talked to householders, posted flyers, and begged assistance from the postman and the crossing guards.

There was a sighting. The woman who called was certain she had located our little Burmese because, she said, "I've never seen a brown cat before, and it had a little white spot at its throat, just like your flyer."

Dale went alone to the vacant lot described by the caller. He sat and waited. In time he saw a small, brown cat, and knew as it drew closer that it was a diabolical coincidence. It was another uncollared Burmese, not show-perfect brown. Like CoCoa, a spot of white marked the place where the pulse beat in its soft throat.

Long hours in the political office filled my weeks. I made more flyers, but it was Dale who spent the daylight hours in the neighborhoods where the little lost guy might be. Then the campaign was over. I cried as we loaded up the pickup.

It was dusk when we arrived home and began to unload, reminiscent of the time Booger made his first overtures to us. I sat on the deck with a bowl of food and called and called. He didn't come. Three nights in a row I waited, but Booger, too, was gone.

Friends arrived. The next morning I said, "Dale, take me to the Pound. I want to get a kitten." I was adamant when he suggested that we wait until our company was gone, so the four of us drove to the County Animal Shelter.

An abandoned five-week-old tuxedo kitten, black mask face and white whiskers buried in my tentative hand, begged me to take him home and pamper him and name him Diogenes. As I headed from the cat room to tell the clerk that I'd been chosen, there were my three companions. A top cage was stuffed full of bedraggled white and black fur.

"This old boy looks like Booger," Dale was saying. I stood on tiptoe and saw the big white head, the telltale black dot under his left nostril.

"This *is* Booger," I screamed, and the rest is history. He, too, was adopted, microchipped, and sent to the hospital for shots and neutering. Dale brought him home in CoCoa's carrier to spend his first groggy night in the guest bathroom. He used the litter box like a gentleman sometime during the night, but howled for release in the wee morning hours.

I gave him food in the house that morning, and a cursory brushing. He gave me a rusty-from-disuse purr. It was a worthwhile trade, I thought to myself as he slipped eagerly out the open back door.

I'll probably spend a couple of hundred bucks a year bailing him out of the Pound, and his jingling tags will add surplus to the bird and mouse population on our property. There won't be any more little Boogers in the hills and barns between here and Idaho. Still, I'm sure he knows we saved his life. He asks in and out of the house as if he owns it, and naps for an hour on our bed if Diogenes doesn't drive him to the door with tom-kitteny earbites and pounces. Today I saw Booger following in Dale's every footstep as my husband did his chores around the property.

Life is good, I tell myself, as I try to train Diogenes to keep his nose out of my face and contemplate upholstering the whole living room in green toweling.

I weep occasionally in the night when I remember it isn't CoCoa beside me, warm in the bed. I rejoice, though, to see the black and white streak of a big, alive, erstwhile tom across our pasture.

It all evens out somehow. Life is good.

PANDORA'S RUMPY RISER

I FELL IN LOVE WITH A NEIGHBOR'S CAT DOWN IN OREGON. It was peach-colored and, to my uneducated eyes, resembled nothing so much as a cross between a cat and a rabbit. Josephine was a Manx, her knob of a tail classified as a Rumpy Riser, and I broke all of the coveting commandments while I lived next door. I determined that my first kitten would be just like Josephine.

Moved to Washington State, I searched and studied. A nine-pound cat book told me how to train, doctor, and appreciate kittens. *Give her a name with at least three syllables,* it said. *Spend two or three of your first days together with the kitten on your lap, petting it and repeating the name. Pet, and repeat the name, over and over,* it instructed me. *She'll come when called when this imprinting is done,* it promised.

The Manx Lady returned my call. "There's no single color peach or orange in this batch," she said. "But I have a little girl tabby, orange and a Rumpy Riser."

Two out of three of my prerequisites seemed reasonable. I went to look, fell in love, and waited five weeks for Pandora (three syllables) to come home.

Home was my new dream house, surrounded by century-old trees and a hundred feet of deck that faced breathtaking views. The eclectic furnishings of my life sat unfamiliarly around eleventeen boxes of books when I went to pick up the just-weaned kitten. I prepared a little cat pan with gentle litter and tied it with a pink ribbon. A low, double food dish in pink ceramic waited for water and little kitty-o's.

She loved it all! I put her in the cat pan as soon as we came into the house so she'd know where it was. Dainty, she stepped out and admonished me. *Yes, I know. I will. Don't worry.* She picked appreciatively at warmly moistened kitten food and looked for a place to nap. In my lap on the sun-warmed deck, we began the imprinting of her name.

Pandora. Pandora. I petted and crooned. We spent every waking moment together for two full days. *Pandora.* The third day she raced to the sound of her name each time I called. On the fifth day, my daughter-in-law visited.

"You've got egg on your face again, Ma," she chortled. "First of all, see this?" She wiggled Pandora's knob of a tail. "If it moves at all, it's a Stumpy."

"Secondly, see these?" She gestured rudely in the direction of the infant's nether regions. "This cat is a boy." She was 110% certain and was never wrong about anything.

What to do? My little tomcat responded to a feminine name. I pondered. The dictionary wasn't unpacked. Under pressure, I could think of only two words that might sound enough like the name imprinted in his diminutive brain.

Ruling out Pandemic for obvious reasons, I picked up the kitten and made our way to the rocker out in the sunshine. He waggled his teeny stump and purred at the top of his tiny lungs as I crooned to him: *Pandemonium. Pandemonium.*

I'M SORRY I WAS TARDY, JACK FINNEY

TODAY, I MADE EGGS A LA GOLDENROD FOR MY HUSBAND. HE loves the dish and thanked me profusely for the tasty white sauce in which the chopped egg swims. As I often do these days, I went to the word processor and wrote a fan letter. It went to the daughter of the woman who taught my 4-H class fifty years ago.

Remembering your mama, I wrote, *and how she taught us to make Goldenrod Eggs.*

I was never able to pander to the famous. Or infamous, for that matter. Rarely could I force myself to stand in line to thank a speaker for his time and his thoughts, even when I was exceptionally grateful for them both. And, on the rare occasion when I did this, I'd see that the celebrity's ears were reverberating with all the *I-me-mys* he'd been smiling at and listening to while the line inched slowly forward. I knew my thanks were going to fall on his anxious-to-retreat and deaf-ened brain, anyway, so I usually didn't bother to get in line.

I've been like this forever. By the time I was fifty years old, I had only ever asked for one autograph. I had collected two, but one of those I stole.

Did you ask whose autographs? Estes Kefauver was the one I asked for and received from that polite, ebullient gentleman. How I admired him and his fearless Crime Commission. Oh, I applauded his race to win the Democratic nomination in '52. That was the year of Estes, Adlai, and Averill. The Democrats were going to get a nominee with an interesting given name, although he'd never, ever be president unless his name was Dwight.

It was a foregone conclusion that Ike would be president, if he decided to run. When he chose to run on the Republican ticket, it seemed as if the heart leached out of the donkey's party. Adlai Stevenson, that grand old statesman, took the nomination by attrition. My guy, Estes, faded from the news.

I have never read a biography of the senator. I don't want to learn that he may have had three mistresses or several illegitimate children or was allergic to his coonskin cap. He was the political hero of my very young womanhood and is sacrosanct there, even if I never told him.

Was there another autograph in my early years? Yes. Richard Armour's. I photocopied it from the back of a Saturday Evening Post check. It was endorsed to a service station near Scripps College in Southern California, where he taught in the early 60's. I was amazed that my light verse hero got small dollars for his work, and that he would endorse anything so splendid as a check from a magazine to buy gasoline. But he did, and it came to me, as bookkeeper, in the cash receipts from our battery route salesman.

Who was Richard Armour? He and Ogden Nash were kings of the snappy, rhymed short stuff you never forget. If you ever quote those quatrains about shaking the catsup bottle or what attracts the mustard from wieners, you're quoting Dr. Armour, although probably crediting Nash. Among Richard Armour's sixty books, full of puns and twisted history, is the series that begins with *It All Started with Columbus*, my all-time favorite fun book.

How I admired him, his nonsense in print all the time, being paid for it an extra bonus. Learning that he accepted checks as little as $5.65 for his work was disheartening, but the minimum wage was then about $1.25 per hour, and how long could it take to write a couple of lines and a title?

Nearly thirty years and much mellowing later, I asked for another autograph. Stood in line, in fact, behind twenty boys of all ages and sizes to get near Wilt Chamberlain. He stretched out in two or three box seats in the old Salt Palace, watching the Jazz play the Lakers. Retired for years by then, he was polite and obliging to all. He gave me a "Thank you, ma'am" when I used my time to babble that I was sure I was the only person in line who had admired and followed him since his college basketball days!

I didn't read Wilt's biography late in the 20th century. It provided source material for every comedian's monologue during its allotted fifteen minutes of fame. I didn't want to hear about his ten thousand women, any more than I wanted to read about them. I guess being the NBA's most decorated center, revered by pro basketball fans in two generations, wasn't enough to sell books.

I have Wilt's autograph on a Jazz program. His soft voice is imprinted on my memory. I get gooseflesh when I watch his innovative play of the game on infrequent NBA retrospectives. It's enough for me, these memories of a basketball hero. But, when I reached the head of the line, I didn't tell him how much his play of the game had thrilled me. What did I talk about? Me.

So who's Jack Finney, and how and why was I late?

I had an ongoing love affair with Jack's work for years, and he wrote one of my five favorite novels, *Time and Again*. It was an alternate Book-of-the-Month selection in the early 1970's.

Several years before that book, I was devouring a magazine under the dryer in a beauty shop. I always needed a fiction fix under the dryer, on the john, at a stoplight. In my hurry to partake, I was often indiscriminate in my selection of reading material.

Thus it happened that, just as I began to think, *This guy writes real good*, I arrived at that awful line. You know the one: *continued next issue*. In my anxiety to start reading *Five Against The House* by Jack Finney, I had missed "Part One of…" And the magazine was already many moons old.

Imagine, if you will, in the age when reading for recreation was becoming passé, the sight of me searching every stack of magazines in the shop, only to find no more installments. The well-coifed, but unread, didn't understand why I was so frantic. I asked for the magazine that contained Part One, and the cosmetician gave it to me gladly, grateful to see me go. With luck, there would be an address for back issues in the pages I clutched to my bosom all the way to the parking lot, *but I wanted to finish the story now.*

And I did, by casually dropping in on stay-at-home neighbor women on my Southern California street. "Hello.

I'm your neighbor at the end of the cul-de-sac. Do you take
Good Housekeeping?" Lahoma Lewis gave me a stack of
back issues that evening. The Finney read was superb.

One day, a box of paperbacks yielded *The Body Snatchers.*
You know how it is when a compulsive reader is getting a
fix: titles and authors are a blur. As long as the cover didn't
portray a haunted house and a fragile woman in flowing
garments, I'd just snatch it up on my way to the privy. A
few pages into this little science fiction book, its memorable
phrasing and great plot points made me stop and look back
for the author's name. Jack Finney.

In 1975, my husband drove through the midwestern
countryside while I read a magazine. It might have been a
new *Saturday Evening Post.* The article, "I Remember Gales-
burg," tugged at familiar heartstrings. I'd already read past
"continued on page…," and had to flip back to the front of
the magazine. Yep, Jack Finney again.

My connection to Finney continued. The tail end of a
lingering illness and a nearly empty container of garage sale
paperbacks were next on my plate. The battered cardboard
box's contents had been reduced to a Pulitzer winner I'd
never been able to finish, Tom Robbins' sweet story, *Even
Cowgirls Get The Blues,* which I knew by heart, and three
Gothics. I chose the least offensive cover on one of the three
and began my read.

"Not half bad," I thought around page 10. "Hmmm?" I
thought at page 20, and turned back to the despised cover,
still contemptuous of its creaky house and bosomy heroine.
The title escapes me today, but the author continued to haunt
me: Jack Finney. I began to think I should write him a fan
letter in care of the publisher of *Time and Again.* I thought

about doing exactly that a couple of times a year.

Assault on a Queen was kind of like *Five Against The House* at sea, discovered in hard cover at the used book store and purchased purposely because Finney was its author. Suspenseful and thrilling to the end, it didn't disillusion me. This man was my kind of writer. I really should get that fan letter written, I thought.

Then there was the short story I read in a mystery magazine while the car was being lubed, some years later. It grabbed me quickly in the old familiar way, and I turned immediately back to the title page. I hadn't run into him for a while. But the author was Jack Sharkey.

Sharkey? Finney? This had to be my boy, the novelist using a sly pseudonym for submission to the pulps. I added a line to the fan letter that lay composed in my head, asking him if he was Sharkey.

In the summer of 1995, the Arts and Entertainment section of the local paper told of Jack Finney's long-awaited sequel to his novel, *Time and Again*. Called *From Time to Time*, it had just been published. I called my local independent bookstore and ordered a copy.

I finally sat down at the typewriter and wrote two pages to Jack Finney. I thanked him for the reading joy he'd brought into my life. The words flowed onto the page as I told him of the chance meetings I'd had with his work over the past thirty years. I'd figured I would get the current publisher's address when the new book came, so I could mail my long overdue fan letter.

Dale picked up *From Time To Time* for me, and brought it home with a big grin on his face. "It sure doesn't take much to make you happy!" he said, as he handed it to me. "Twelve dollars in paperback!"

The fan letter, typed now and waiting only for the envelope to be addressed, lay on my desk. I picked up my new book and looked at the back cover.

Published by Scribner Paperback Fiction, it said. *Jack Finney is the author of more than a dozen books*, it informed me. *He died in 1995.*

SHOES AND LIES

IT IS THE LAST DAY. MY HUSBAND HAS COME FOR ME. Sunshine, now that I am escaping. Drizzles during previous days incarcerated me indoors with them until their parents returned from work.

Dressing for school and for day care will be child's play this morning, I think. It's the last day.

I notify the young one that the only shoe he's wearing is on the wrong foot. "I don't care," he smart-mouths at me, lying back on the littered carpet with his hands under his head, defying me to care.

"Well, so don't I!" I'm at my best at their level. I jam the remaining shoe on the other wrong, stockinged foot. The golden cherub protests the outrage. He kicks and screams.

"No! No! I wan' my shoes on the wight foot! I wan' my...I wan'...."

He wound down, hiccuping, and gazed helplessly at the shod feet stretched out in front of him. He was trying, no doubt, to figure out which was the 'wight' one. I left him to his hefty decision, as the schoolgirl now needed inspection.

"I'm gonna take this to school today, Gramma!" She flapped the miniature bong around her neck. I'd seen it last night. It blew bubbles, endlessly. Kindergarten would ban the family in perpetuity if she took it to school. I was gentle.

"No, honey. It's not for taking to school. Take it off, now. Thanks." She was complying as Grandpa lumbered to the kitchen looking for coffee, ecstatic at having missed the babies' breakfast.

We are ready—they for school and the sitter, we to race across the Cascades to our four-legged children. "Don't forget your backpack," I say to the tiny student, and stop short. I was once six years old.

"Where is the bubble pipe, honey?"

Her tongue was prepared, but her eyes didn't have the hang of it yet. They strayed covertly to the backpack as she replied, "I guess I must have taken it downstairs."

I insisted I had to check her backpack for the library book that needed to be returned this morning, and she gave up with a shrug that said, *Oh, well. I tried.* I removed the toy and did not lecture, for her mother had also been six on a Wednesday morning long ago.

"I hadda take 'em off because I had a big hole in my sock!" The angel boy had the last word as he sent me for another sock. I lined up the right and left shoes in front of him on the carpet. He always knew I would.

On the road, I tell my husband I should have lectured about the lie. "It's a bad habit," I insisted, "and not respectful."

He was magnanimous. "All kids lie, dear. They outgrow it. This kid isn't even very good at it. I wouldn't worry."

He'd only been with them a few hours, and most of those hours he was asleep. Of course he wouldn't worry.

I brought the big, holey sock home with me, darned it soft and perfect, and sent it back across the mountains.

A few weeks later they were over here visiting. The kids were getting up, and my muse and I were at the word processor, when there was a small noise behind my right shoulder.

"Fiss it, Gramma. Fiss it?"

There was the beautiful boy waving a tiny white sock with a grey heel and toe. It had a small hole in it.

So we went to the mending sack and got darning thread and needle and 'fissed' it, and a matching one of grandpa's as well. Keith was properly impressed, and I was nearly grandmaternal. It was a Kodak moment, one I hope he'll remember, since I am a confessed bad grandma, and there have been so few.

Stranger

728 Marine Drive N.E.
Tulalip WA 98271
Thursday night, 9/26/02

Dear Dorcas Leigh:

We finally discovered why all the outside cat food was disappearing, and Booger wasn't getting any fatter! Here we'd been blaming Mollie, the 80-pound redhead from down below, whose Golden Retriever taste had already shown itself to be more on the side of Science Diet nibbles than Iams' chunks for dogs. But we knew there was a Stranger in our midst when Artemis spent the night outside, and the early morning deck was covered with fur. Chunks of our youngest's white, Siamese fur.

Stranger grew more bold and appeared on the deck in the daytime a couple of days later, checking out the areas where food and water often sit. Battered for his age, he had one raggedy ear and ribs that showed through his dark tiger-stripe. Inside, our four-legged kids howled at him and cowered, but Stranger stood his ground until a human walked outside. His skedaddle was nothing short of lightning-swift, and his obvious masculinity was the last sight human eye had of him as he leaped from the deck.

"Gone forever," we said.

Gone for two days, actually, and he was nearly tomcat of the walk when he appeared again. Only Pandemonium would go outside, and he skirted Stranger with obvious respect. I asked the neighbor lady whose cat it was, and her reply was that someone had probably dumped it. She'd already asked around.

"Maybe the other boys will get used to him," I told my husband.

"No, *no*, NO!" His usually gentle voice was fervent. "He has to go to the Pound."

"Okay," I promised, and let Stranger see that it was I who put a small bowl of dry food and a dish of water out for him. He barely waited until I was back in the house, so hungry was he. He inhaled everything.

A week went by, and Stranger continued to eat the meager portions I placed outside for him, while our own little guys were all practicing to be house cats. I patently ignored him when he came to the settee where I sat smoking on the deck, even though he rubbed against my legs and purred like a motorboat. *A smart cat*, I thought. *He probably wants larger meals.* When he stopped rubbing and started scratching himself, I got paranoid about fleas. He was so well-behaved; he thought rubbing the flea-treatment cloth over him was lovin', and he was starved for it.

Now he wanted to go in the house, and Dale wanted to give him a ten-foot running start. "If you can't have a kitten,

Judith, what makes you think you can have an abandoned tomcat?" So, tearfully, I agreed that he had to go to the Pound.

On two succeeding days, hardhearted Mr. Nakken was "too busy" to take Stranger to the Pound, as he had threatened. On the third day, he came home with news.

"The Arlington No-Kill Animal Shelter has reopened, Judith, after some great financial difficulty. Their number is in the book. Call them and make arrangements."

I blackmailed Sue into taking him that same day, by telling her my husband would take him to the Everett (kill, *kill*, KILL!) Pound if I couldn't get him into her newly reopened facility. So I lured Stranger into a cat carrier with food and became just one more human who done him wrong. At the shelter, Sue put him in a temporary dog crate with food and water, and the last thing I saw was his sad eyes peering at me through the wire. Dumped again, they said.

I'm going to go visit him as soon as I can drive! In the meantime, we all made a donation to the Arlington No-Kill Animal Shelter. Diane and I each put up twenty bucks, and we thank you for your contribution, my dear Dorcas Leigh. Your tax-deductible receipt is enclosed.

Yours very truly,
J. R. Nakken
Arlington Animal Shelter's
Newest Fund Raiser

PANDEMONIUM REVISITED

PANDEMONIUM IS GONE. HE WAS THE FAVORITE OF MY FOUR-legged children, and my heart hurts. He was angry when I brought the little girl-kitten, Catalina, home from the farm. Thirteen-year-old Booger cuddled her, while Artemis, the last baby, taught her racing games, but Pandemonium aimed his stubby Manx tail in my direction all month and hissed at her.

I missed playing our game. Before Catalina arrived, Pandemonium would consistently retrieve the tinsel ball I tossed each morning while I drank my coffee. Friends marveled at a cat that would fetch.

At last, he forgave me. One morning, he begged for the ball, and we played for a long time. He stayed in the house and slept on my chest that night. There was a wild storm the next day; Pandemonium went out and never came home. I couldn't stop crying.

Yesterday morning, half-grown Catalina was bedeviling me as I drank my coffee, so I tossed a crumpled piece of paper to distract her. She trotted back and laid it at my feet.

Amazed, I threw a soft toy farther out. She retrieved it, too, and stood below me, searching my face intently. Last night she slept on my chest.

I am comforted.

FLOWERS FOR ALGERNON'S GRANDMOTHER

I CREATE HAPPY STORIES TO MOLLIFY MY KILLER TEMPER. Twice I attempted mayhem and worse before I turned my life around, and it was just a matter of time before I offed someone with the car or my little handgun. So, many years ago, I got rid of the Beretta, saw a shrink, and practiced the anger management tricks he suggested. But I invented the story idea myself and still use it today, although I don't need it as frequently in this new millennium as I did in John and Jackie's thousand days.

It works like this:

A healthy six-footer races me to the checkout stand, perhaps actually clangs against my grocery cart. I was probably no match for him even before osteoarthritis and sciatica began their joint attack on the quality of my life. Do I stand behind his load of beer and sausages and seethe, raising my blood pressure with visions of what I'm going to do to him? I do not.

His dog's just recovering from a lengthy illness, and he had to leave her in the car, I tell myself. He needs to get back to the parking lot *poste haste* and is so glad I didn't raise a fuss. I grow warm with self-sacrifice and practice of the Golden Rule, and my heart rate stays at 62.

Or (taking into account that this scene is not currently possible because cataracts have canceled my drivers' license and left me house- and garden-bound.):

A little red car races past me on the right and squeezes me nearly off the freeway entrance. Do I run him down or even show him one of my educated fingers? I do not.

His wife's about to give birth, and he's so grateful that I moved over for him. Because of my kindness, he'll make it to the hospital just in time to see his first child emerge. Probably he'll remember me in his prayers for many months.

They come to me out of the blue, these stories, and they make me happy.

Toward the end of summer, we went across the mountains to the daughter's for a weekend. Returned home, watering the garden and planters I'd nurtured since spring, we discovered two pots of New Guinea impatiens missing. They're dear to my heart, these flowers that were seedlings and are now in the full essence of their Seattle summer beauty, and I was angry.

Some kid lifted them for his grandmother, I told myself immediately. She's even more housebound than I am, and was overjoyed to get the scarlet blooms in their clay pots from the grandson she doesn't often see. I even named him and was content with my make-believe.

Two weeks later, we were away overnight and returned to find a wooden planter full of impatiens and tall green spikes missing from the display under the hundred-foot maple in our secluded yard. It was the pride of my garden, and I cried and shook before I got back into the earlier tale.

"You ain't seen nuthin' yet, Grandma," was Algernon's response when she thanked him for the first two pots. "Wait until you see what I'm bringin' you next time!" I even managed a chuckle at the humor of my story's second chapter.

Last week I had my first cataract surgery and wasn't out of the house five hours. A huge clay bowl of geraniums, lobelia, and marigolds was missing from the upper deck when I returned. This third violation was so near the rooms where I eat and sleep and write that my anger was overlaid with fright, but fear was soon dispossessed.

"Please take the target chamber off your Ruger, dear," I instructed my husband. "Mount the cylinder with the magnums."

Algernon's grandmother has enough flowers.

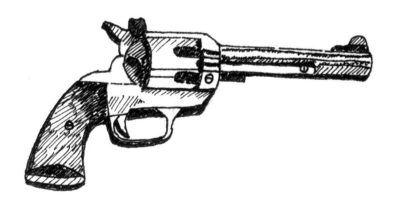

ON DEPRESSION

THE BATTLE ENDED IN THE THIRTY-FIFTH YEAR OF MY sobriety, its last two decades more of a quiet, armed truce. In those last years, I could hit my bed of an evening, right with God and the world, and sleep without dreams. Still, the morning light might find the black stuff of doom and despair hovering above my head, and all I wanted to do was pull the pillow over my face and sleep forever. I didn't bow down to the whim, of course, but it wasn't always that way.

Many of us, recovering from alcoholism, discover that we have been afflicted with clinical depression most of our lives. So-called normal folk recognize situational depression—a loved one dies, divorce happens, or the post-partum blues come to visit—and they sympathize when one of these things happens to trigger it. But of the worst of it, the black abyss of mornings, they don't have a clue.

Blanche did. "Don't make decisions when you're de-pressed," my mentor advised when I was six or eight months sober and wanted to quit my little job or move to Dallas or go blonde.

"I'm not depressed! I'm just (sick) (mad) (broke) (disgusted) (worn out)...." Fill in the blanks. She said I was a classic case of clinical depression and that many recovered alcoholics suffered from it. Chronic depression was usually worse in the winter, she said. She would pray about it, since I still pounded tables defending my atheism. In the meantime, I was to plant some flowers. No, she didn't care that the snow was knee-deep to a point guard outside. I was to get some of those little peat pots and seeds and start some flowers in my kitchen. In my gardening ignorance, I chose carnations, hard to grow in our locale.

Many others had these terrible blues, I kept repeating to myself, and didn't have to drink or break things or scream at the kids. It comforted me, as did the tiny seedlings when they popped through the mesh-covered peat. I nurtured them with fervor. Work, my sober club, teenagers, and guarding the fragile greenery on the kitchen counter filled my winter, but did not dispel the awful black cloud on days it chose to envelop me.

"I'm so depressed," I told the doctor as I visited for the ongoing urinary tract infection that was a residual of my drinking career. "So depressed that I don't know if I'm really in pain or just that—depressed."

He didn't even look up from his desk, this man who was the first 'outside' person I ever told of my addiction to alcohol. Each time I had to visit him, he would ask, with a twinkle in his eye, "How's our other little problem?" Now I realized he didn't really know me at all.

"We'll fix up that depression right now," he declared, writing on a prescription pad. I declined, since the club old-timers were vocal about even prescription drugs unless it was life and death, and I didn't think I was that bad.

Carnations by the bushel graced every potluck I attended that
second summer of my sobriety, and every woman's desk in my
small office displayed a frequent bouquet. I even decorated
birthday cakes with them, their spicy mélange of orange and
white so brilliant against chocolate icing. No weed lingered
more than a day in their long, narrow bed against the high
cedar fence that separated us from our unknown neighbor's
dark and shuttered house.

I talked to my flowers. "Lookin' good there," I'd croon,
as I cultivated with the little green garden tools I'd bought
on sale at the hardware store. "Good baby! You're gonna pop
those buds in another day. Good job!"

Blanche had another bright idea, right before the tulips.
"Put tomorrow's shoes under the bed tonight," she instructed.
"While you're down there, it couldn't hurt to say a few words."

So when Indian summer was upon us, and I couldn't
bear to pick the few remaining blooms, I began to talk to a
Creator in the morning before I looked out the window for
a dwindling shot of carnation joy. It wasn't easy, but "thanks
for no depression today" became a frequent part of those
talks. Sometimes, it was just "thanks that it wasn't so bad,"
and often it was "I don't have anything to say today," but I
learned to pray while finding my shoes.

"Tulips, now," she announced during the week of the
first frost and last carnation. The catalog she handed me was
bursting with reds and yellows and purples. Hyacinths! I saw
hyacinths on one of the first pages and longed for some for
my soul. But I still had the long, dark, cold winter to conquer
and bemoaned the wait. Oh, she laughed at me.

I didn't know they were planted in the fall, nurtured
beneath the snow by Something I was beginning to trust.

Which was more exciting, planting the different sizes of oniony brown bulbs in the pattern supplied by the seed company, or seeing the first November snow gently blanket the corner that would soon be a blaze of early spring color? How can I describe the first sight of pale purple braving March's lion weather, my very own crocus heralding the fact that winter, too, shall pass? Was it just beginner's luck that every bulb burst forth in its preordained color, leaving no gap in the picture I had painted with tulips, daffodils, crocuses, and hyacinths? My stone cold heart, which had begun to soften in the past months anyway, melted away.

"Good job, God," I said during that morning's search for shoes.

A bad one was upon me that Saturday morning, a May day when the ground was warm enough to work around the emerging carnations along the fence. It was going to be a tough few days, I knew. I had fussed with the fifteen-year-old and hid in the bathroom to hide my tears, then escaped to the back yard to try and compose myself. I spoke to the little green shoots. "You really do come back, year after year after year, don't you?" Comforted by tilling the sweet-smelling earth, I wasn't even startled by the tentative voice above me.

"Are you having babies in there again this year?" The neighbor's face above the fence was a mix of bravery and fear as he ventured to converse with me, and looked as if he were prepared to leap from whatever he stood upon if I rebuffed him. "What kind are they?"

Don't scare him, came the voice from Somewhere. He sat on that side of your fence all last year and heard you loving your flowers, and never said a word. Depression went on a back burner while I had a quiet, minute-long conversation about my first flowers. Depression nearly disappeared when I went back into the house and said my sorries to the dear daughter. When, on Monday morning, Neighbor Man left his house at precisely the same time I did for the first time ever and returned my wave, depression was gone.

Six more seasons passed, seasons of tulips, of carnations, of learning about the ripple effect we homo sapiens have on one another. In the early years, those seasons included infrequent days of depression, accompanied by lots of self-pity.

"I'm doing everything right, aren't I? And I was sure the last time was going to be just that—the very last time!"

Blanche was loving but unsympathetic. "It's all in God's time, Judith, not yours."

I met and married my soul mate and learned the joy of caring for another at least as much as I did for myself. Introspective inventory of my day's action became my routine before retiring. My neighbor nearly hugged me when I took some carnation starts to his front door before we moved, but settled for a pat on my shoulder and a shy farewell smile. Does he think of me as often as I think of him, I wonder, this young man who was the first recognized example of my effect on others?

My mother died. Too young, too beautiful, too stupidly. I raged and sank into the abyss, pillow over my head. But I couldn't stay there, not even for a day. I was serving as treasurer for the club to which I felt I owed my new life. I had to go to the post office, get the contributions, write receipts and notes, keep the books, and pay its obligations. I slogged through it because of my duty and didn't realize for a couple of years that it was part of the plan for my life. God knew I had to be 8½ years sober and in service to others before a horrible life jolt such as this one could happen to me. My trust—my faith, if you will—grew stronger.

But what about depression medication, you ask? My answer always was:

I don't believe you can learn the fear of Antabuse and the love of sobriety at the same time, and I feel the same way about conquering depression. I developed some tricks: If the black cloud was there, I jumped out of bed immediately, saying my prayers on my feet. I resisted the longing to skip a shower and clean clothes and instead bathed, dressed, and did my makeup with extra care. Then I plastered a smile on my face and went to face the day.

If it wasn't a workday, I cleaned the junk drawer, the cluttered linen closet, or the basement laundry area. Hateful jobs, but I wasn't going to feel any worse, so why not get them done? Often, good feelings crept through the molasses morass of my mind when I took a later peek in the closet or drawer, or washed a load of clothes. Once, the kitchen ceiling, unscrubbed for five or six years, actually cured a tough bout of the bad blues. It took my aching arms all weekend, at the end of which it was gleaming. And so was I.

Hesitantly at first, I began to talk with others who might be afflicted. Months would go by without an occurrence, and I would begin to hope it was forever gone when another black morning would arrive. There was a reason for this, I now believed. Maybe it was just so I could share my experience with the newly sober, the confused, to see the look of hope on their faces when I said, "Oh, yeah. I've had it for years. But how I am today is about as bad as it gets, anymore."

Complacence arrived in the guise of contentment. My soul mate was disabled and took to house-husbanding like a duck to water, I thought, while I spent more and more time on my career, less and less in the service of others. I knew it all, at sixteen years clean and sober, and had the world by the tail. One morning, I awakened to find myself alone in the house. Divorce papers soon followed.

It was a deeper, darker place than I had ever been. I kept waiting for it to pass, for I had handled tough situations before. I didn't stop to think how I had been resistant to my nightly inventory for some weeks before the black hammer dropped, and I was soon paralyzed with depression. Work was out of the question, the mail piled up, mice invaded my house and nested in my new sofa. I had blackouts—sober blackouts. One night, a blue light flashed behind me and I began to pull over, only to realize that I was driving in the far left lane of a four-lane state road. I "came to" another evening in a forest thirty miles away and didn't know why I was there until I found the coil of garden hose I had taken with me. My mind wanted suicide, though I did not.

What if I succeeded the next time, or the next? My daughter, just a mile away with her own little family, would be scarred for life. Already overburdened with my illness, she would surely blame herself. "If I had just taken the kids over that day," she would say. Or, "I should have taken Mom to the movies," or any of a myriad after-the-fact mind excursions anyone takes when they feel they've been neglectful. I just couldn't do it to her and was afraid I would.

I found a shrink. "I've had a lot of recovering people," he said. "Most of you won't take the medication you need." I assured him I would do anything if it were a means to an end, that end being my recovery from this hopeless state of mind. I don't think it was a con job, his explanation of the clogged channels in my brain (was that why my head felt like slow motion cotton?) and the synapses that didn't spark. The medication would clear the channels, he said, and I need not take it forever. I took it for five months, and it worked as he said it would.

Since that dark time, I have studiously allotted my times of introspection, prayer, and meditation into each day. When I close my eyes at night, my slate is clean, or I will clean it first thing in the morning. I say, "Thank you, God," often during the day and increasingly less often, "Forgive me, God."

Still, a day or two of depression, invariably in wintertime, continued to happen. I persevered with bright lipstick, smiles, junk drawers, and kitchen ceilings, and by sharing with others afflicted that "this is about as bad as I ever get."

I unburdened myself of my errors of commission and omission to a young woman who was unhappy with the man she loved and did not want to leave. In tears, I urged her to work on her own spiritual path and build on the 95% of her husband that she adored. "If I had done that," I said, "I would still be married to my beloved."

That night, I got on my knees. "I have tried not to question, God, but now I think I see why. My experience is meant to benefit other women. It's a large price to pay, Sir, but I am accepting it. Thank you for my life." Healing was complete when the phone rang in my twenty-fourth sober year, hundreds of miles and seven years away from my soul mate. We were remarried that Thanksgiving. Blanche, gone now, was surely beaming down and repeating: "All in God's time, Judith. All in God's time."

Another alcoholic woman, sober for many years, had depression episodes as severe as my worst one was. We began to meet weekly, discussing and practicing spiritual tools with emphasis on introspection and daily inventory. Life got brighter for each of us, and then the winter loomed. "What else can we do?" we asked each other. So we made a pact. If it was there when we awakened, we would say a prayer quickly, go right to the phone, and call each other. I prayed for both of us that night, and the love of one depressed drunk for another prevailed. Neither of us called for that purpose, all winter long. The phone was there, but we didn't have to use it.

So what's my solution, you ask? Is it flowers and clean junk drawers, inventories and prayer? Is it the depression buddy system, illustrating once again that we can do together what we can't do alone? For me, it has been all of the above, plus this:

My God has a daily plan and purpose for my life, and I trust with absolute certainty that there is a reason I didn't step wholly into the bright sunlight until the thirty-sixth winter of my sobriety. If that reason is only to share my experience, strength, and hope with you, it is sufficient unto this day.

ON FORGIVENESS

THE PUBLISHER IS PUTTING THE BOOK TOGETHER, AND I HAVE only alluded to my stepfather, the story unwilling to be written. How does one depict her childhood's bogeyman without the tale becoming a self-pitying story of perceived atrocity after atrocity? Where does the narrative begin, and how does it end?

He was left-handed, like me. How I hated that analogy! Born in the last decade of the 19th century, his dominant hand was tied behind him in his one-room Iowa schoolhouse, and the only writing he could produce in his adult years was a right-handed, illegible scrawl. He seemed to hate me from the moment he married my mama, when I was nearly four, and knew only one method of discipline. He beat me, the precocious weird kid, with belts and yardsticks and climbing boots for every real or imagined nonconformity. My body bears half-century-old scars from abuse that would have jailed him today, and it is certain that the battering of my mind produced blemishes far more life-threatening. How could I write of him?

My mama gave me his World War I diary when she was
dying. "Read about him when he was young," she urged me.
A glance at the chicken-tracks that passed for handwriting
was enough for me to tuck the slim leather volume away
in a drawer. I was forty and believed my life was sober and
straight enough to forget about him. Now painfully aware
that I had married several men twenty years older than I in
a subconscious search for a father figure, the red rage rose
in my throat each time a memory of him flitted across my
consciousness. I couldn't, I wouldn't try to read the diary. I
would always hate this man.

Early on in my recovery journey, a time came when I had
to 'fess up to the wrongs I had inflicted upon others. A myriad
sins of commission and omission existed, all stemming from
my basic character defect: Walled up and shut in by nature
as well as by nurture, I had charged through life as if others
did not exist.

"What about the stepfather," my mentor urged, but I
didn't need the prodding. Already I had realized the inhu-
manity of my last confrontation with him. In his bed, dying
of cancer on a hot summer day in 1954, he was the ghost of
his robust Scandinavian self. The end was so near that my
mama sat with him day and night, and I grudgingly spelled
her at the bedside so she could get some fresh air. He had no
breath to speak with, but his eyes, so huge in his shrunken
face, pleaded with me as his lips formed the words. Sorry.
Sorry.

I turned my back on him and faced the door until Mama
returned. There would be no deathbed repentance on my
watch, in my eighteenth year.

Yes, I was mortally sorry for my cruel act. Today, I would
not do such a thing, I stated in the stilted letter I burned in

the fireplace a quarter-century later. I considered forgiveness accomplished. I did the best I could, though I still hated his memory.

A few seasons of contentment passed. Time really does generate healing, and I could engage in conversation about him at the occasional family gathering without shaking. One day, a secretary brought me some papers to sign.

"Your handwriting is so fine," she remarked. "Most left-handers write illegibly, upside-down, or both."

I started on one of the tragicomic tales of my childhood. "My wicked stepfather made me write," I began, "the minute I got cursive writing in school. An hour a day after school and two hours in the summer, I had to write." I was going to go on about how he'd rip up what I'd copied from storybooks if it didn't suit him and make me do it over again, and conclude with "at least I reaped some benefit from the torture," when I was struck silent by awareness.

He wanted me to have better than he did. He was ashamed that he couldn't write.

I wrote another letter for the fireplace that night. *Thank you for my fine handwriting*, it said. *Please forgive me for my final cruelty at your deathbed*, it continued. *I have no conception of who or why you were, but may you rest in peace.*

As the trickle of smoke went up the chimney, my hatred disappeared.

Thus it was, at the dawn of this new millennium, that I dug through boxes carried unpacked from city to city, to unearth his diary. I would gain insight on the man, I thought, in order to write of him for my book. It took me three weeks with a magnifying glass to decipher and transcribe the thirty-six small pages of entries ranging from 25 July 1918 to 6 April 1919, and my manuscript is littered with notations of "illegible." At the end of my task, although I knew more about him, I still didn't have a story.

He had no imagination, no vision, no awe. A twenty-five-year-old, married draftee who had never been out of Iowa, he traveled across country, shipped over to France, saw sights of which most of us only dream, and what he wrote most about was menus. A passing mention of the Statue of Liberty in New York Harbor, and a paragraph extolling the virtues of the ship's lunch. One half line for Black Jack Pershing, and three for the chicken dinner that day.

There are no entries from 8 November 1918 to 28 November 1918. Recovered in the death ward from the Spanish Flu that killed millions (the toe tag with his vital statistics is tucked in the little book), he recuperated in New York City in the old Siegel Cooper department store, transformed into a military hospital. Ambulatory, he was taken to Broadway plays, the names and stars of which I do not know, only that the crustless sandwiches served were kind of dry. The last entry in the diary is brief: *Got in Storm Lake (Iowa) at 9 AM today.* I want to believe he was so overjoyed to be home that I will never know what he had for breakfast.

I guess that's the story.

ON WINNING

Judith Viorst was my favorite female writer, and it had nothing to do with our being blessed or cursed with the same given name. Probably about my age, she was emerging as a writer in the late 60's at the same time I was knocking at the entrance door to the human race. I found her first in a *Redbook* column, telling of one of her fierce Jewish sons.

"We don't have Christmas trees and gifts because Christians believe Jesus was the messiah, and we believe he was only a very good man," she had explained to the youngster.

"Aren't I smart," the boy replied in all innocence. "Even when I was first born, I knew that Jesus was not the messiah, but only a very good man."

My kind of woman, with her sly and philosophical humor probably lost on the bulk of the masses. I reveled in her slender volumes: *It's Hard to Be Hip Over Thirty* and the subsequent *Forty and Other Atrocities.* She got me for life when I discovered *Judith Viorst's Dictionary,* for this woman's belief system was exactly like mine on the subject of winning and losing, to wit:

*Winning: It's not whether you win or lose,
    it's how you play the game.
Losing: It's not whether you win or lose,
    it's how you play the game.
Playing the Game: Play to win.*

Judith knew how I felt, I decided. Refusing to participate in anything I couldn't be best at was the way of my narrow life, even years after my liberation from alcoholic obsession.

Jo Del Kimbrell answered our ad for a bookkeeper-accountant. Hers was one of many interviews in the attempt to find a "young J. R. Nakken," so I could move on to a new branch office. She alone seemed to fit the bill and was a cutie to boot. Under five feet tall and built like the proverbial, albeit miniature, brick outhouse in her size zero trousers, Jodie went on a diet if the scale read 100 pounds, jogged before it was the rage, and was a whiz with the numbers. I moved on soon and often. Over the years, she was to reenter my life on occasions when I needed accounting help, and she was between jobs. Thus it was that she was doing some temporary work for my new employer and me while I reorganized the administrative staff.

"I need a favor," she twinkled at me on the third day.

"Anything," I replied and meant it.

"Well," she said, making a little face and shrugging her shoulders, "I'm entered in this bicycle marathon in Montana, and I'm riding five miles every morning for training. I just don't have time to get showered and get all the way over here unless I get up at 4:00 AM. Could I come in at nine? You're always here late, anyway."

"Of course. But, bicycle marathon? Montana? Why?"

"Well," she explained, "I've never done it before, and I want to."

"Good reason," I applauded apathetically, busy at my desk. "What do you get if you win?"

Her countenance was matter-of-fact, her perfect little hands picking dead leaves off the purple hanging plant in the corner beside her. "Oh, I won't win."

Did I sense that my life was about to change in the next millisecond, or was I just aghast at my protégé's non-competitive attitude? Whatever the reason, I stopped sorting the morning's mountain of paper and challenged her. "What are you doing it for, then?"

Five words were her answer, five words that were to cause me to look to the end of my life. Those words set me on a path whose goal was to live each day as if it were my last, and to live my life as if it would be forever. Five words.

"I just want to finish."

ABOUT THE AUTHOR

J. R. (Judith) Nakken, always a closet writer, has been a good bookkeeper and bad barmaid, a practicing alcoholic, accountant, recovered alcoholic, Avon Lady, administrative director of a large recovery facility, comptroller, and, finally, a full-time writer. *Stream and Light* contains memoir pieces written and stashed away over a 25-year period.

Her first novel, *Three-Point Shot,* for young adults, won a Writer's Digest award in 2004, and she delights in speaking to youth who are using the book in their classrooms. "American Patch," included here, won first prize in the Preservation Foundation's 2003 contest. Ms. Nakken currently resides in what she describes as "God's Country," on the Tulalip Indian Reservation north of Seattle, with her soul mate, Dale, and an assortment of eccentric felines.